What Are They Saying About Death and Christian Hope?

by
Monika K. Hellwig

PAULIST PRESS
New York/Ramsey

Library of Congress
Catalog Card Number: 78-61726

ISBN: 0-8091-2165-4

Published by Paulist Press
545 Island Road, Ramsey, N.J. 07446

Printed and bound in the
United States of America

Contents

Preface

Many good Christians no longer know what to think about death, judgment, heaven, hell, purgatory, life after death, praying for the dead and praying to the saints. There is an uncomfortable feeling abroad that what we used to be taught does not hold anymore and that there is nothing to take its place. Moreover there is an awareness that not much is being written or published that seems to help solve the problem of this gap.

In fact, published writing on what theologians call individual eschatology (which deals with questions such as the above) has been very scanty for some decades. There seem to be basically two reasons for this. The first reason is that there has been an important shift of attention to some urgent questions in what theologians call general eschatology. This last is concerned with what Christians hope for the human community as a whole. It is concerned with hope for the world, and therefore with questions as to how worldly our hope can be.

This has been a shift not only in eschatology but in the whole of contemporary theology. German Protestant theologians, chiefly Juergen Moltmann and Wolfhart Pannenberg, have pointed out that the Gospel of Jesus Christ, the message of the Christian churches, is not primarily concerned with the past but with the future. It is primarily concerned with the promise and vision of the coming reign of God, in which all creation and history is to be fulfilled and consummated. As understood by these authors the Christian message is therefore in the broad sense a political message. It is a message about what is possible in human affairs in the public as well as the private sphere—a message that implies far-reaching criticism of the way the world is now run and further implies a challenge to reconstruction. The work of these Protestant theologians has been complemented by the "political theology" of Catholic German theologian J. B. Metz which has emphasized the challenge to action and the institutional Church as the instrument for public, broadly speaking political, action proportionate to our Christian hope. It has been complemented further by the "liberation theology" that has emerged as a school of predominantly Latin American and predominantly Catholic theologians, and has attempted to engage the issues of Christian hope for mankind on the practical basis of contemporary third world problems.

In view of all this activity, it is not surprising that there has been less published in the area of individual eschatology. But there is a second reason for the dearth of new writing in the field. There has been a fairly rapid assimilation during the last few decades of a more sophisticated understanding of what we can know in such matters and how we can know it. Along with this understanding has come the realization that we have been accustomed to dealing with the traditional teachings on "life after death" with little attention to literary genre. As a result some of the presentation and explanation may have been too literal-minded, deflecting attention away from the real intent of the teachings. Whenever there is a moment of discovery like that in theology, it seems that theologians "run for cover" because they need time to think in peace, try out some new interpretations and check them against all the data of Scripture and the traditional Church teachings. This kind of thing may take many years before some individuals begin to publish and many more before any kind of emerging consensus appears.

Some such individual writing has, however, already been done in these years. The focus has not been a speculative one, addressing itself to the nature of heaven, hell, purgatory, after-life, and so on. It has rather been a practical and existential focus, addressing itself primarily to death and the Christian community's experience and testimony of the resurrection of Jesus. This short book deals with the insights and reflections of some of the principal theological authors who have written in this field recently, particularly with insights given in the writings of Karl Rahner, Ladislas Boros and Roger Troisfontaines on death, in the writings of F. X. Durrwell, Louis Bouyer and H. A. Williams on the resurrection, and in those of Karl Rahner, Hendrikus Berkhof and Gregory Baum on the interpretation of the traditional symbols of eschatology. However, it in no way attempts a survey or overview of contemporary individual eschatology. It is the author's personal synthesis, indebted particularly to the authors just listed.

The content of Christian hope for the individual has, of course, been discussed through the Christian centuries. It is a new problem, however, because our changing awareness prompts new questions about the content of Christian hope that have simply not been asked this way before and therefore have not been answered before. In response to these new questions, this book gives what may be in some ways new answers. The intention, however, is to demonstrate that it is a coherent unfolding of the old answers, faithful to the revelation that we have from the beginning in Jesus the Christ.

1
What We Would All
Like To Know

Death is mysterious. It is not an aspect of our human existence that we can easily take for granted. Even those who habitually deal with dying patients in hospitals seem to have considerable difficulty coping with the death of others, and seem to find many ways of avoiding a real confrontation with death. Death is not only mysterious but threatening. This is not only because it is usually associated with pain. Many other events are associated with pain, such as surgical operations and childbirth, but people come through the experience to resume their normal lives and tell us about it. People do not die and come back and tell us about it. There is a lurking anxiety about annihilation, about a terrifying darkness in which one might simply cease to be.

The first point we would all like to know about death is just exactly what comes "after" or "beyond" it. We would like to know how things will be, what to expect. We would like to be prepared. This is, after all, the way we have all learned to live. Growing up means leaving a kind of paradise-existence of early childhood, in which we could live in a timeless and unmeasured present. We have to measure time when we accept responsibility, when we plan and prepare for "the next thing," when we know we must be "on time."

Most parents have to spend a great deal of energy keeping their children aware of time—time to pack up the games and come to the dinner table, time to tidy the room and go to bed, time to collect coat, cap, gloves and satchel and leave for school, time to be dressed for church. Most children resist being constantly hassled out of their happy present and being pushed through the hoops and doorways of a time-frame imposed from elsewhere, not from their own inner needs and drives. But as they begin to accept it all as inevitable, they try to cope with it by interiorizing the time-frame and the patterns. While these are completely alien they are nothing but pain and frustration, but the child soon discovers a certain freedom in knowing what the next transition will be, when it will be and how to be prepared for it. This is why most of us have heard our children express anger and frustration by saying, "But I didn't know it was Sunday and we had to go to church, and now you've spoiled my game." "But you didn't tell me it was going to be dinner so soon and I was just having such a good time." "Well how could I know it would take so long to tidy up?"

The need to interiorize the time-frame and the problem of achieving it do not end in childhood. It is typical, not unusual or abnormal, that the college student and the graduate student and the professor are still constantly trying to interiorize the schedule and the calendar, to anticipate the demands and the pressures, to budget the appropriate time for reading a book, doing a piece of research, writing a paper. It is typical that the professional worker, the executive, and even those whose work is more readily measurable are caught by the constant need and effort to grasp and appropriate shifting time-frames and demands in order to be prepared and be able to manage.

Most of us most of the time are more or less seriously threatened with losing our grip of the patterns, being overwhelmed with alien demands and slipping into painful chaos. The challenge of death comes into our human consciousness, shaped by this constant orientation to a future we must anticipate as accurately as possible in order to be prepared. But death frustrates this orientation because we cannot see what is beyond. Sometimes Christians have not been completely honest with themselves about this. The stark reality is too easily evaded by saying, "Jesus has been there and Jesus has been raised from the dead on the third day and has returned to tell us about it." Just what Scripture and tradition have passed on to us from the teaching and testimony of Jesus about hope for the individual beyond death will be presented in Chapter 3. It does not answer the question implicit in the human thrust to interiorize the time-frame.

In our times, as in most times in history, there is another way that people try to evade the challenge of death as presented in this first point. There are always attempts to peep beyond the darkness of death through the testimony of those who have been "clinically dead." Earlier generations did not use this term, but were well acquainted with the idea that people had been observed to be dead and had then returned to life and told what they remembered of the "other side." Such testimonies are collected, for instance, in *Life After Life* by Raymond A. Moody, Jr. (N.Y.: Bantam Books, 1976). While the author's claims for this book are modest, the book has been widely acclaimed as proof and description of after-life, of the being of God and more. However, testimonies such as these do not tell us anything about what is beyond death. They do not decribe the definitive transition from the life we know, because they do not come from people who have made that definitive transition. In fact the testimonies themselves all describe a hovering in an inconclusive way at the periphery of our ordinary human experience, ended by a return to the ordinary mainstream of human experience. What these testimonies do tell us is a great deal about the experience that leads up to death and a great deal about continuing consciousness after the point at which people have already been pronounced "clinically dead." The testimonies do not tell us anything in response to the desire to anticipate what is beyond the definitive passing out of this life.

There is a third way that people avoid this question of what lies beyond death, and this third way must be taken seriously, if only because it has such a long tradition of Eastern wisdom behind it. However, it is not a Christian answer to the question of what lies beyond.

It is the teaching about the transmigration of souls or their reincarnation. According to this understanding, what lies beyond is a succession of further life cycles of the kind we already know, perhaps including animal as well as human options, perhaps determined by merit in previous lives, or perhaps determined by personal choice prior to each incarnation. In our times, some Western Christians claim that this is not incompatible with Christian teachings. This claim is discussed in Chapter 3. However, most traditions that teach the transmigration of souls or reincarnation make no claim of continuity of reflexive self-awareness, and the question that most of us want to ask is, "What will happen to my reflexive self-awareness beyond death? Will I continue to be reflexively self-aware, and under what circumstances?"

The second point we would all like to know about death is whether and how we can control what happens beyond death. This is related to the question whether there is ultimate moral accountability and "what the rules are." In the ordinary patterns of our lives we try to gain freedom and personal equilibrium not only by understanding the time-frame and demands of the world in which we live, but also by trying to control them. Since childhood we have all been conducting experiments in building the world, the structures and expectations of society our own way. Again, most of us have had revealing experiences of this with our children and have faced announcements such as, "This is my house and you all have to do as I say." "Anyway, I don't have to do as you tell me." "I'm not going to school today, and that's final." "Children don't have to do the cleaning up; only grown-ups should have to do that." This annoying litany is an experimental procedure which in one form or another continues through the rest of our lives. We experiment to find out how much we can restructure things to our own specifications and still get away with it.

Not all cultures and societies set as much store by this endeavor, but our competitive society, which constantly urges us to be upwardly mobile in the patterns of domination, teaches us to value ourselves largely by how much and how effectively we can control people, situations and material resources. We are conditioned to think that things are getting better when we extend and intensify our control and when we are progressively becoming independent of the control of others over our destiny. This may well be one of the factors most profoundly undermining marriages in our times in our society. It is certainly a factor that makes the second question about death appear as a rather different question from that which was asked in earlier times.

In all societies and at all times there has been some concern with personal destiny in relation to death. Usually it has been assumed that there is a moral exigence in human life sanctioned by consequences that reach beyond death. This has usually been seen in terms of a ready-made, predetermined system guaranteed by divine ordinance. The only way human persons could be concerned was to try to find out as much as possible about this predetermined system and how it worked. In other words, one had to find out the code of behavior by which one would be judged. In this perspective there is really very little sense of having control over one's own destiny or a future reality. This perspective reflects what has been most people's experience of this world as they knew it—their experience of their own existence between birth and death. Through most of history, most people have found themselves in this life placed in a predetermined slot in the social structure, with predetermined tasks. Choice has extended only to the question whether to play the assigned roles willingly or reluctantly or to rebel and be punished. Human questions about death and what may lie beyond death have certainly always been formulated in terms which our experiences of life have suggested, and the pattern of predetermined structures and allotted roles seems to have dominated the thinking. Even today, of course, most people in the world, including those of our Northern Western society, do not experience life and society in any different way than that described above, but what makes the difference is the rising and spreading tide of very different expectations. Very few significantly shape their own lot and destiny in this world, but all are taught to aspire to such creativity.

Because of this changing focus in our experience there are subtle and far-reaching changes in the way we ask the questions about the ultimate destiny of human persons. On the one hand, we have been taught by the rising tide of expectations to want so much more. On the other hand, from the actual frustrations of most people in the face of these rising expectations, we have learned a pervasive pessimism that undermines even the more modest hopes and expectations of former times. The question is no longer that of discovering the "rules of the game," but a question as to whether there are any rules, and whether ultimately goodness is rewarded at all, and whether there is any meaningful definition of goodness. In other words, present-day questions about individual eschatology tend to be questions about whether life makes sense at all, and whether we can really know that it makes sense or only pretend so because that in itself might be rather helpful.

This sobering movement has caused a response in Christian theology. What has been written about individual eschatology in the last several decades has been very cautious about trying to decipher the symbols of hope. That has left one area of concern—that is, the consideration of death itself and of the process of dying. Karl Rahner,[1] Ladislas Boros[2] and Roger Troisfontaines,[3] as well as a number of authors who contributed to the *Concilium* volume *The Experience of Dying*,[4] have reflected on the questions we are all asking, but have interpreted them as questions about death rather than questions that bypass (or even in a sense deny) death by asking simply about an after-life. The basic question, as all these authors see it, is how we are to make sense of life in the face of death and what the Gospel of Jesus as the Christ tells us about death and about the meaning of human life in face of death. Questions about the shape of our hope as it transcends death are all seen as rooted in the need to grapple with death itself. Therefore, not only philosophical reflection on death, but also studies arising from a psychological and therapeutic contact with the dying, such as the work of Elisabeth Kübler-Ross,[5] have become important for the theologian dealing with individual eschatology today.

The starting point for consideration of death has moved from the abstract proposition that all human beings must die to the concrete instances of the experience of dying to the extent that we have been able to witness them. In this shift another question takes precedence over those concerned with after-life. The question that is then first in order of business is: Why must we die? This question in practice, in the experience of those confronted with the rapid approach of death, may begin as a petulant protest but soon becomes a serious existential quest for a personal and fully integrated consummation of one's own life.[6]

When we take seriously not so much the philosopher's question about the death of all living beings but rather the dying person's question "Why must I die?" we enter into a new realm. First of all, we discover that this question has far greater existential and spiritual depth than any questions we may ask about after-life. That is because questions about after-life too easily spring from idle curiosity that involves one's whole personal stance very little. The question "Why must I die?" engages all one's values, self-definition and commitments. Secondly, therefore, we soon discover that this is a question about life, about the whole meaning of human existence, and not only a question about one moment at the end of life.

Most of us prefer not to think too much about death. It appears as something morbid, mentally sick, when someone dwells on death at times when death is not imminent. Contemporary theologians have suggested that our unwillingness to look at death may be seen as an aspect of sin and its distortions of our whole view of reality.[7] We would like to pretend that the question does not concern us. In fact, however, when we do ask the dying person's question seriously we are likely to discover that it sharply and correctly formulates a pervasive, inarticulate question about our own present experience. Death is not only a point at the end of life but a dimension of our whole experience of living. Besides the clearly recognized need and task of becoming independent, acquiring control, understanding, managing, organizing, harnessing nature and shaping the future, there is a less recognized and certainly less valued need and task. There is the need and the task of learning to accept dependence, to relinquish control, to trust without understanding, to adapt oneself to the managing and organizing of others, to accept the ways of nature and to be open to the uncreated and unpredictable future. There can be no genuine service or community, no art or contemplation, no family or friendship, no peace or security without this complementary aspect of human life. Nevertheless, we experience this aspect of living as some sort of diminishment of what we are and of what we can be. The serpent's insinuation has lost none of its immediacy. It always seems as though we could be like God by the assertion of unsituated, unconditioned freedom.

The question "Why must I die?" turns out to be the most immediately relevant question for all of us at any stage of our lives. To acknowledge that the center and meaning of reality is not in one's self, but immediately in human community and ultimately in God, is that aspect of life which is consummated in death. To learn to move off the center of the stage, to make room for others, to cooperate with plans not of one's own making, to serve a cause that reaches beyond one's own lifetime and benefits others, is to be about the business of dying now. There is a certain necessary and wholly constructive process of the "centering" of the self when a person progressively accepts responsibility, acts consistently and purposefully, and forms personal values and opinions that eventually coalesce into a philosophy of life. But alongside of this there is a necessary process of the "uncentering" of the self. The self must become the center of responsible action, but it cannot be central in the purpose or goals of the action. To be a body is to be part of a process and interaction that is much greater than oneself, and to be spirit is to be focused in attention, love and service away from oneself, to others and ultimately to God.

The question "Why must I die?" is a sharply focused way of asking the more pervasive question, "Is the uncentering of my self really necessary?" In philosophical abstraction the question is interesting but not disturbing. In the concrete it can be quite painful. It is the question of spouses in a marriage. It is the question of parents in face of the unlimited demands of their children. It is also the question of siblings in a family, rivals at school or work, companions in any cooperative venture. The question "Why should I accommodate myself to you, or wear myself out for you, or compromise my plans for you?" always turns into the very exigent question "Who am I, and what is the purpose of my existence?" This in turn is the humanizing question that makes us take stock of ourselves and appropriate our own being and destiny.

2
What We Can Never Know

A question that is urgent and has been neglected in the first chapter, concerns the nagging fear of annihilation, of being snuffed out. This has been left to the present chapter because it requires a discussion of the area which theologians call "the hermeneutics of eschatological statements." This imposing and sonorous phrase simply means: how one may interpret statements about the ultimate destiny of the individual and of the world. During the last few decades this has been a matter of special concern to Karl Rahner,[8] Dutch Protestant theologian Hendrikus Berkhof,[9] Anglican theologian H. A. Williams,[10] North American Catholic theologian Gregory Baum[11] and others.[12]

There is a subtlety in religious language in general and in the language describing the content of Christian hope in particular. We build our language directly out of our experiences. When we are talking about something that we have never experienced, we use vocabulary created by those who have experienced it and we try to understand what they mean by analogy, that is, by comparisons. When we want to talk about something that has never been experienced by anyone because it has never happened yet, or has never been experienced by anyone who lived to tell us about it, the challenge is greater. What we do in fact is to express ourselves in two different ways. We express what we intend or hope for the future by a negation of some things in the present that we know and experience. The slave says, "I will be free, and that means no more chains, commands, exhaustion for some-one else's profit." The inventor says, "I will make a flying machine, and that means it will not need solid support from below." In some-what the same way the believer says, "God will welcome us into the kingdom of heaven, and that means no more war, poverty, suffering, death, fear, separations, crushing work, disappointments, loneliness." The other way in which we attempt to express such elusive future real-ities is in the language of poetry, a language that hints and suggests by images and visionary dreams. To interpret poetry literally is almost always to trivialize it and quite miss the point. About the future we quite frequently use expressions like "waiting for the sunshine after the storm," "coming out of the tunnel," "expecting a bed of roses" and "finding the rainbow's end." The reference in each case is to something meaningful enough which cannot, however, be said with precision or described concretely because it is not known with preci-sion or concreteness.

Such is religious language and more particularly the language concerning our Christian hope. We try to say so much more than we can ever put into words, and we even try to say so much more than we really know or understand. We try to express experiences that elude language, and hopes that are greater than any precise formu-lation that we can find. Therefore we express them by negation of all that has to be overcome and cancelled out, and we also express them by poetically worded dreams and visions of a happy future.

Such language and such images are not peculiar to Christianity. All the great religious traditions of the world have such ways of speak-ing of the future outcome of human life. When we look at the different forms these expressions take, one thing becomes clear. The images used are culturally conditioned. That is, it is from our past and present experience that we try to glimpse or project a future. The "absolute" future that represents our expectations beyond death and beyond his-tory as we know it is no exception to the general way that we always try to project the future. Thus, while it may seem very strange to us, some quite traditional societies which have not fostered an intensely individualist self-awareness have produced very little imagery to express the individual's expectations beyond death. Evidently many societies in the history of the world in the past found that they did not really need to deal extensively with the question of what happens to the individual who dies. People were not asking this question persistently and with anxiety. Rather they were asking what would happen to their children and their children's children, and what would be the fate of their people and their clan. In our culture we are inclined to think of this "we-consciousness" that predominates with traditionally oriented peoples as something primitive and not fully human, and yet we should ask ourselves whether it is not really more human. Certainly, it is growth toward maturity when persons are able to look beyond themselves to be concerned with others. Certainly, community, trust, love and common achievements of all kinds are heavily dependent on some progress toward self-forgetfulness.

In the Hebrew experience before the time of Jesus, and in the preaching of Jesus and the early generations of his followers, community images of the future tended to overshadow the individual images. These images seem to refer not so much to another place than the world we live in, as to a transformation of the same place. They refer not so much to a realm outside time and outside the history we know, but rather to a fulfillment and bringing to completion of all that is yet in conflict and struggle in the history that we know. They are images of a land of plenty and peace and deep harmony among peoples, images of a feast, a great celebration and so on. These images are quite earthy and concrete, and reflect the culture and experience out of which they were born. It is only with the increasing influence of Platonic philosophy and Gnostic interpretations of human existence and human experience that the images become much more ethereal. Platonic philosophy tends to see the "really real" as somehow not in space and time, but transcending them. Gnostic ways of thought see the human person as essentially a spirit imprisoned or detained in a body. The effect of these two strains of influence on Christian images of hope for the future has been to devalue the concrete, the social or community dimensions, and the actual course of history in the world, as well as all the bodily dimensions of experience.

As a result of these factors, later images expressing the hope of Christians for the future became much more individualistic and certainly more unearthly. The resurrection from the dead, which had a very strong communal character for Jews at the time of Jesus and for Jesus and his early followers (as is evident in the New Testament), began to fade into the background and give way to the teaching of the immortality of the soul. Christians, influenced by the thought currents around them, were interested in the question "What will become of me when I die?" Moreover, when they asked that question, what they meant by "me" and "I" evidently was the spirit or consciousness which they took to be the essential self in the accidental body. In response to the questions that were asked in this way, the image was that of the soul being released, so to speak, from the imprisoning body, and then continuing its existence without being much changed. The ordinary context of time is assumed to be left behind, and a quasi-time substituted. Space is pictured as being left behind and a realm outside space substituted. In this realm, it is assumed, there will be a quality of experience dependent on what has been "earned" in life. There will be full happiness, or total misery, or some sort of transitional phases between these.

The language by which our traditional representations express the threat of total misery is the language of fire and burning and physical pain. The language, on the other hand, in which the hope and promise of full happiness is expressed is far more elusive and ethereal, for we speak of the beatific vision. Literally understood, this simply means the looking that makes happy. The result of the difference in style of expression is that for most people the images of "hell" are far more meaningful than the images of "heaven." This is obviously unfortunate. It means that attention is drawn not to the content of Christian hope, but to the obverse side of it, the deprivation that threatens. In other words, there is a tendency to ask the questions about the future from a perspective of fear rather than one of hope.

However, there are other problems with these images of expectation of the future. While they were set in a way of seeing the world in which much was wonderful, awe-inspiring, and mysterious, the images served well. Whether they were earthy like the resurrection and the banquet or feast, or rather ethereal like the continuation of the disembodied soul and like the beatific vision, the images convey a sense of expectancy of something much greater than has been expressed, something ineffable. But our Western culture moved into a very different and quite restricted phase of consciousness. We began to equate truth with the empirically verifiable, and to lose interest in whatever could not be demonstrated. In this context the language of eschatology became a much less confident language. Teaching about Christian hope was put on the defensive, and too often made the same assumptions as the culture at large concerning the equation of the true with the empirically verifiable. Unwilling to allow that Christian teachings on eschatology should appear as false by the current criteria, believers (and even teachers of the Christian tradition) seem to have used the traditional formulations as though they had been literally intended and were in fact empirically verifiable at least in principle.

Such a shift in the understanding and presentation of the traditional teaching must certainly have seemed a gesture of certainty and confidence, but it has had and is having the opposite effect. If the images and formulations of our eschatology are understood as poetic, imaginative projections out of the promise and exigence of our present in the light of our past experience, then the formulations of the teaching appeal to our participation in a personal, living and creative way in the always new and vital expression of the hope of the ancient community that is also truly our own hope. On the other hand, if the images and formulations are taken as literal presentations of demonstrable truths, they are alien and alienating, because we know well enough that we cannot demonstrate their truth and have not seen it demonstrated and do not expect to see it demonstrated. In other words, the most important aspect of our Christian vision and commitment, the content of our hope, then becomes something that is thought of as quite clearly predetermined and specified in some alien realm to which we have no access. It is then a matter of accepting someone's word for it that things are this way beyond death and history, exactly this way. Sooner or later the question arises as to who said it and how it could be known with certainty then if it cannot be verified now.

Contemporary Christians come to these questions, having been conditioned to expect and be concerned about the survival of the disembodied soul. The question is formulated, "What happens to my reflexive self-awareness when I die?" We are so accustomed to this formulation that it may be very difficult to see it as culturally conditioned, and certainly not the only or even the most obvious way of reflecting about the challenge of one's own death and the exigence that that challenge places on the whole of one's life. The way we have been taught by our culture and by the established formulations of Christian hope to think about death and about our personal future tends in our present setting to cause a deep-rooted anxiety and fear about annihilation. It is the fear that perhaps life is, after all, absurd. If the perfection of everything that human life and personality strive for is achieved in the reflexive self-awareness of the individual, then all hope and expectation is sharply focused on the fate of that reflexive self-awareness. Conversely, all dread and anxiety is also focused on the loss or destruction of that reflexive self-awareness. Consequently, there is a certain pressure to satisfy oneself of the demonstrable truth of the immortality of the soul, but this satisfaction cannot be had on the terms on which it is sought.

Even as we struggle with this we are already being overtaken by a new wave of consciousness suggested by our changing culture. We no longer think in simple dualistic terms of a soul living its life inside a body. Modern physiology and psychology have restructured our image of the human person. They have brought us to a realization already suggested by Thomas Aquinas in the thirteenth century, but not really taken seriously in Christian theology in the centuries since. This realization is that the soul is the "livingness" of a living body. In other words, soul, spirit, self-consciousness, is rooted in and emerges from the physiological functioning of the body. We are living bodies, living a uniquely complex and reflexively aware life. The reflexive awareness reaches a critical point at which we can partly escape the process of conditioning and predetermining of our actions and existence by outside forces. As our bodies grow and we develop motor skills and speech, the capacity for intellectual and spiritual activity expands and offers certain possibilities of freedom. But we have no experience of intellectual and spiritual activity that is not rooted in physiological functions of the brain and nervous system.

This has some devastating consequences in our expectations of the absolute future, that is, the future beyond death. It means that in our present phase of Western culture, when we are all very much influenced by the sciences, we are losing the "image" of the human person which allowed us to think about the survival of a disembodied soul. If the soul is the livingness of a living body, and not a distinct entity somehow inserted and contained in the body, then one cannot easily think of the soul as lifted out of the body to continue its separate existence. That separate existence has been reduced to an absurdity, an impossibility, a "category mistake" in our thinking. It then becomes almost as unthinkable as the proposition that the apple indeed must rot and disintegrate but at least we shall still have the redness of the apple in the bowl on the table. In fact we are reconciled to the realization that the redness of the apple survives in our memory alone.

This changing consciousness and changing image of the human person has helped to intensify and to focus the question whether death means annihilation of the human person. If the person is the living body and we can observe that the living body decays and breaks up to become the substance for other organic things that have their own life and their own quality of livingness, then one cannot easily predicate the survival of the person beyond death. What contemporary theologians have done[13] is to consider whether there is a unique quality in human existence that makes the analogy of the apple inadequate. The question has been raised whether human consciousness, rooted in and emerging from the physiological functioning of the human body, nevertheless so intensifies and frees itself from the limitations of that body that in death it reaches a "take-off point," so to speak. Thus, it has been suggested that if the dying dimension of life is the dimension of self-gift to others, then what happens at death might be conceptualized in terms of a transition of consciousness from being rooted in the individual body to being rooted in the community. In this perspective, death would be seen as bitter frustration and destruction by the sinful person who is selfish, self-centered, domineering, self-willed. On the other hand, death would be seen as consummation by the redeemed person who is fully turned toward others in love and service, who is centered in the transcendent God, whose creativity is responsive to the divine creative initiative, who is "tuned in" to manifestations of divine purpose.

This kind of interpretation of dying certainly commends itself on biblical grounds. It can serve as an explanation of the serene deaths of the patriarchs. It also hints at the meaning of the death of Jesus, which is presented as such an ecstatic consummation, transcending the tortured agony which was inescapably real nevertheless. This kind of interpretation of dying also offers some directions for meeting the challenge that death presents to the living at all times. It even suggests possible ways of conceptualizing the resurrection, which will be discussed in Chapter 6.

Nevertheless, this interpretation does not answer the questions prompted by curiosity nor those prompted by the anxiety that expresses the sinful element in all of us. It is an interpretation that offers an orientation, not one that gives any information. It only serves to underscore that there are questions we continue to ask to which we can never know the answer. It serves to underscore the fact that no amount of thinking, research, or wishing can take away the finality of death. We can exert ourselves to obtain a clearer picture of all that happens up to the moment of death. Beyond that we can make projections which by the nature of the case are not verifiable. All that we can know is whether they help toward a more integrated and more redemptive way of living or not, whether they confront the issues or evade them.

In terms of our usual expectations, this state of affairs is highly unsatisfactory. Contemporary theology seems to suggest that Christian faith requires a reversal in this process of evaluation. We might approach the matter in a different direction and discover that in face of the ineluctable reality of death our usual attitudes and expectations are highly unsatisfactory. Death reveals our need of redemption because it challenges every inauthentic stance.

3
What the Catholic Church Teaches

It may seem to some readers that the foregoing is all irrelevant speculation, because the main question for a Christian believer is what the Church teaches in the matter. As explained earlier, however, there is more than the usual problem of interpretation in the field of individual eschatology because the official teachings left poetic language with all its imagery intact, while theological reflection has until very recently tended to take the imagery and symbolism rather more literally than it appears to have been intended when first formulated. For this reason contemporary scholars such as Josef Neuner[14] and Karl Rahner[15] have carefully scrutinized the accumulation of official teachings[16] in order to penetrate beyond the apparent literal sense to the spiritual and doctrinal meaning of the utterances.

In order to understand Church definitions, decrees and symbols of faith (creeds), it is usually necessary to ask first, "What was the question at issue?" This may involve a long and intricate historical quest. For some readers the resulting theological discussion becomes tedious. To others it seems disingenuous, seeming to twist the texts to our present prejudices. But the endeavor is an important one in the context of a Catholic understanding of revelation, tradition and doctrine. The Catholic understanding is that the official pronouncements of the Church in the past still stand, through changing eras of cultural experience and technological and scientific developments, giving us

cumulatively an unerring guide to the interpretation of the Gospel of
salvation in Jesus as the Christ. To stand within a Catholic frame of
reference is necessarily to take these past utterances seriously, no matter how tedious the search for their meaning. To be consistent and
loyal within Catholic tradition, however, it is neither necessary nor
particularly helpful to teach such utterances naively without reference
to their historical and cultural context.

Briefly stated, the official eschatological teachings of the Catholic
Church which have been solemnly defined are the following.[17]

1. The death of the human person as we actually know it is the
consequence of sin. It is seen as something not appropriate to human
existence. This, of course, is maintained in the context of the Christian
teaching from New Testament times that Christ has conquered death.
Though it does not become explicit in Church documents, there is evidently an underlying assumption that to live in Christ is also in some
measure to transcend the tragedy and absurdity of death.

2. Death involves an inescapable judgment which leads immediately to the definitive outcome of each person's life and decisions. This
statement arose in the context of a definition of death as the separation
of the soul from the body. This was assumed to be a temporary separation ended by the resurrection of the body and the reuniting of
body and soul. In such a context there were some logistical problems
in conceptualizing what happened in the interval between. Actually,
the particular conceptual framework of time outside and parallel with
historical time was part of the cultural presupposition and not part of
the definition of faith. Therefore the main problem to which the pertinent statements[18] were addressed appears in other cultural and conceptual contexts as a non-problem. Nevertheless, the notion of a "particular judgment" of the individual at death is an important one.

It is at this point that one may raise the question of reincarnation
and its reconcilability with Christian faith. Reincarnation implies that
there is always another chance to make good. The Christian teaching
seems to imply that all is at risk in a human life, and that the fundamental options taken become definitive at death, leading either to con-

summation of all that human existence means or to its utter frustration. It is true that the possibility of purgatory, a further process of purification or integration, is included in the list of possible outcomes. However, there seems to be no suggestion that the purgatory of the Christian teachings is a second opportunity to make the fundamental life options constructively in charity. Rather, purgatory is presented as the completion or fulfillment of options already made and not fully implemented, and as the completion of the process of reversal of options repented but not at the time of death completely withdrawn in all the complex and far-reaching consequences they may have had in human living. Moreover, the inexorable teaching of the possibility of final damnation, seems to undercut any possibility of reconciling the notion of reincarnation with Christian teaching.

It must, in all fairness, be reiterated here that there is no way of proving which teaching is right to the satisfaction of an "objective" or disinterested bystander. It is only possible to say that the two teachings seem to be irreconcilable. Moreover, in the interests of fairness, it must also be said that in terms of its consequences in the life-style of the believer, the doctrine of reincarnation has much to recommend it. If the conditions of the next life are depicted as consequent upon behavior in this life, there is a sanction for moral exigence. At the same time, if the next life is depicted with a strong strand of continuity with the present, there is a certain support for the kind of detachment that is very serene in the face of tragedy and of death. Out of this kind of detachment great courage is sometimes born. Unfortunately it is also true that such a view of the ebb and flow of life through successive incarnations fails to hold individuals ultimately responsible for their actions, and allows a certain callousness toward the suffering and the oppressed. These latter are seen as working through the consequences of previous choices and actions they themselves made, and as having it in their own power to move into a better life next time. Not only one's own suffering and frustrations, but also those of others are relativized and reduced to a very small scale. From a Christian point of view this appears as a severe problem, though it must be said at once that Christians have often done something similar by placing the content of their hope totally and unequivocally beyond death. Such a conceptual scheme also allows one to be casual about the sufferings of others, no matter how extreme.

3. The fulfillment of a human life, heavenly beatitude, consists of the direct (or unmediated) vision or enjoyment of the very essence of God, going beyond faith and hope, overflowing in bodily delight. It is the fulfillment of all human aspiration but also much more than human existence really leads to (supernatural). There are degrees of this happiness but it is definitive; it cannot be lost and it is forever. Such happiness is attained by those who die in the favor of God (grace), that is, by those who die in a disposition of love (charity); it cannot be attained this side of death. The fullness of this beatitude is possible only because of the breakthrough made by Jesus Christ. Those who pass over into this beatitude of fulfillment are not lost to those who remain behind in history, but are in communion with them and able to help by their intercession with God.

It should be clear that most of the vocabulary used here is either very broad in meaning, such as beatitude/happiness/fulfillment, or frankly metaphorical such as heaven and vision. In other words, it does nothing to satisfy anyone's curiosity about what may lie beyond death. It reaffirms images of hope from the Bible and from Christian spirituality traditions. It roundly asserts that human existence is meaningful, not absurd, and moves toward a great fulfillment. More than that, it insists that that fulfillment is not only for others who come after us, our children or others who inherit the consequences of our choices and actions. Rather this fulfillment is offered to each human person. None is relativized to an historical process in which others are the actors or subjects of history while this one is used and expendable as part of the process.

Such a collection of affirmations about ultimate human fulfillment also links it to the core of human existence. Heavenly beatitude as depicted in the Church documents is certainly not something arbitrarily added on to earthly life. It is not casually linked to the events of earthly life by observance of rules and rituals in a special preparation-for-after-death compartment of living. Rather, heavenly beatitude is presented as the outcome of a total life orientation. It is presented as more than is implicit in the nature of human persons, not by way of an addition but by way of a transformation of the whole being. Even though the expressions used are generic, metaphorical or really quite circular in their definitions, some very significant points are being made, and these points transcend the particular cultural and conceptual context in which they were first formulated.

4. There is a purgatory or "place" of purification for those who die in the grace of God but without having put everything right in their lives. These are people whose salvation (their destination in heavenly beatitude) is assured at death. Its deferment by a state of suffering is temporary. They remain in communion both with those who have attained heavenly beatitude and with those yet living the present life, and they are helped by the prayers and intercession of both groups. The metaphor used for the purification they suffer is that of fire.

Clearly, these teachings are not a literal description of facts, but a profession of faith in the justice and mercy of God. Protestant scholars are wont to point out to Catholics that there is really no direct biblical warrant for the statements in the preceding paragraph—a point that must be conceded. It is not, however, in conflict with the biblical projections of hope in Jesus Christ. This is an area of the expression of faith and hope in which the continuing experience of the Christian community certainly demanded further statements in response to new questions. As we learn in the rather stylized stories of the Acts of the Apostles, the community of believers soon learned, apparently much to the scandal of some of them, that conversion to God in Jesus Christ does not happen instantaneously in its fullness. Christian life continues to be a struggle with many setbacks and betrayals, and death overtakes most of us when our affairs are not entirely in order and we are not yet fully converted. Any simplistic notion of a judgment at death that fully vindicates if it does not fully condemn cannot long survive observations from experience. It cannot deal with the scandal of the unfinished life-project.

Taken as a whole, and allowing for space and time metaphors, the doctrine of purgatory both moderates and reinforces the teaching of the ultimate exigence of the "particular judgment" of each individual person at death. On the one hand it moderates this teaching by removing what might be an excessive anxiety about the extreme difficulty, even impossibility, of attaining salvation, inasmuch as there are always remnants of selfishness even in the lives of very loving and generous persons. Quite early in Christian experience, people exalted the martyr's death because it seemed most like a death of total and consuming love, willingly and quite deliberately chosen in conformity to the death of Christ. Such deaths were exalted, however, precisely because they were not the rule but the exception. Moreover, Christians were unequivocally taught not to volunteer for martyrdom as it was presumptuous to arrogate this sublime calling to oneself. There seems to be an implicit admission in this that many Christians do not reach perfect charity. In response to such a realization in the community there had to be some reflection and some agreement on the authentic teaching concerning the outcome for believers who die with unresolved contradictions in their lives. The doctrine of purgatory is precisely the response that emerged.

On the other hand, the doctrine of purgatory also reinforces the teaching of the ultimate exigence of the "particular judgment" because it attacks any minimalist understanding of what is required for salvation. It denies the notion of a "pass/fail" basis for the particular judgment, in which a positive balance of charitable behavior in a person's life would mean that the unresolved contradictions would simply be "overlooked." This way of thinking would make salvation essentially extrinsic to the reality of the person. In the existential reality of personal becoming, unresolved contradictions are not simply "overlooked." They keep returning to vitiate the personal project until they are dealt with. It is too facile to project into and beyond death cheap terms for personal integration and maturity which we well know simply represent an evasion of the reality we experience before death. Purgatory seems to underscore this. Everything is really at stake in the making of a human person. Death confronts us with the ultimate exigence. There can be no evasions. What has not been coped with before death must still be confronted and fully worked out.

The question has sometimes been raised whether the teaching about purgatory necessarily has reference to a time-span (or a quasi-time) after or beyond death or whether it might be referred to the very moment and process of death itself. Clearly all the time language that we use concerning beyond death is metaphorical. We are transposing a dimension of historical experience. Any claim to measure time outside history can only be metaphorical. What is beyond death we cannot know in this way. An interpretation of the doctrine of purgatory that places the process of purification within the process of death itself certainly has much to recommend it. Death necessarily completes the project of self-surrender as well as the surrender of property and of power—power over others, power to shape the future, power over one's own fate. What happens in the death of another is never in fact within our perception. We see only some of the events that lead up to death, and may be privileged to share some of the dying person's reflections, feelings and responses in that time leading up to death. The crossing over itself is necessarily and forever undocumented and unwitnessed.

5. Both theologians and Church authorities have been preoccupied from time to time with the question of the fate beyond death of those who through no fault of their own die without faith. There was through the ages a rather persistent sense that persons who grew to adulthood could not help but be confronted with the fundamental exigence of God on their lives, no matter what the religious or non-religious language used to express this exigence. Though the explanations varied, the predominant sense of the tradition seems to be that all adults are sooner or later, perhaps even at the moment of death itself, confronted with the call to, and opportunity for, faith, hope and charity in response to the saving God. Therefore the question came to

be considered mainly in relation to infants. It would seem that the answer given in the course of time, limbo (in the margin), rightly designates the state of the question rather than the state of the children in question. In other words, when all the answers are added up, the mind of the Church teachings seems to be: we do not know what happens, but we do know that God is just and merciful.

6. Human persons really can damn themselves. To die rejecting the favor (grace) of God is to perish irrevocably, that is, forever—to burn in unquenchable fire. The main emphasis of the statements that insist on there being an eternal fire seems to be on the totality and the irrevocability of damnation. As mentioned already in this chapter, the Church documents seem to spring from an overwhelming concern to convince Christians that to be human is to be ultimately and totally responsible for the outcome of one's own human becoming. Looked at from another angle, this is an insistence on the reality of freedom, not only as a privilege but as an obligation.

Contrary to what is sometimes supposed, the cumulative sense of the Church documents does not suggest a literal interpretation of the "fire of hell."[19] The term is certainly metaphorically intended. Fire is a powerful and much used symbol in human experience. It represents the experience of being consumed, but this can be positively or negatively evaluated. We speak of being consumed by the fires of love. We represent the Holy Spirit of God in the Pentecost scene in tongues of fire. Fire is a symbol for the prayer of mystics. Yet we also speak of being burned up with anger. We represent the vengeance of God with the fire that consumes Sodom and Gomorrah. Fire becomes the symbol for punishment or frustration beyond death. Both kinds of analogies are suggested by common usage. Incense is burned, but so is trash. A simple clue to the symbolism of fire may be this: it is the destiny of the human person to be consumed for others; if it happens by way of a willing self-gift it is ecstatic joy, but if it happens against a self-serving and self-centering struggle it is ultimate frustration. The "forever" of these definitions of Church teaching seems to be intended to underscore this irrevocability and totality, rather than to assert anything about a time structure outside history and beyond death.

7. All of the foregoing in Church teaching is set in the context of an expectation of the consummation of the world and of human history. Christ is to come again in judgment, consummating all things and initiating the eternal reign of God. The dead are to rise in their bodies to meet him and participate in that final and general judgment. There is much to consider in the teachings concerning Christian hope for the outcome of the world and its history,[20] but it will not be discussed here because the subject of this book is that of individual eschatology. The topic that is of immediate concern in this paragraph in this context is that of the "general resurrection" which is dealt with in the following chapter.

4
The Death of Jesus and the Resurrection

As was mentioned in Chapter 1, the first question of individual eschatology in the order of experience is: Why must I die? As pointed out in Chapter 2, the Christian answer to that question is given in the death of Jesus which Christians see as an overcoming of death. As will be clear from Chapter 3, Jesus, who was crucified and is risen and glorified, is seen in Christian faith as the judge and criterion of the goodness of others at their deaths and in the ultimate consummation of the history of the world. The Christian understanding of the death of Jesus is at the core of Christian hope, and it is this focus which is being emphasized anew by those contemporary authors who deal with individual eschatology.[21]

The starting point is the ambiguity of death and of every question about death. If we look at death simply as a biological phenomenon, it appears as natural in the lives of human beings in the same way as it is natural in animal and vegetable life. It appears as natural both physiologically (with reference to the growth and maintenance patterns of the individual organism) and ecologically (with reference to the interdependence of living organisms for nutrition). Christian teaching, however, as already pointed out in Chapter 3, point 1, maintains that human death is a consequence of sin. There appears to be no intention of asserting that human lives would have continued through unending time, maintaining themselves physiologically and endlessly repeating the rhythms of work and play and sleep. When we try to imagine such an existence, most of us do not even find it attractive. It has been customary, rather, to speculate that if it were not for sin, persons would pass on into the fulfillment of their being, into a more intimate union with God, without passing through the trauma of death.

The question would appear to be concerned with what it is that makes death an experience of frustration, fear and defeat, rather than an experience of passing on into fulfillment. A superficial answer to this might be that it is the physical pain associated with death and particularly the possibility of its untimely occurrence that render it so frustrating and threatening. Yet sober reflection on experience shows that the fear of death does not recede with age nor in situations where death is expected to be swift or painless. Moreover, the classic event of the martyr's death underscores the fact that there are issues more deep-rooted than the question of pain and the cutting off of a life in youth. The martyr, the one who chooses to die for a cause—whether this person be a Japanese kamikaze pilot, a freedom fighter, an illegal conscientious objector to war, a Marxist radical social critic or a Christian saint—has in greater or lesser measure appropriated his or her own death as personal act. We know from history that the death that is chosen for a cause is often, by the decision of others, a terrible torture death, and that the one who nevertheless chooses to die it is often young enough to be surrendering great unactualized possibilities. From the testimony of those who have been close to them we also know that those who have so chosen to die frequently manifest an unexpected transcendence of physical pain, fear, the sadness of loss, and the urge for revenge. Those who witness it are not infrequently overwhelmed with the sense that such dying persons have attained a certain maturity or perfection of what it is to be human.

When Christians look with awe and even worship toward the dying Jesus, their perception is that here is a revelation of the fully human and through it a revelation of the divine. This revelation should not be seen apart from the context of martyrdom in its broadest sense. Christian piety and reflection appear sometimes to obscure the issue as presented by the apostolic witnesses to the death of Jesus. Piety sometimes focuses immediately and almost exclusively on the divinity of Jesus and thereby presents him essentially as immortal, but evokes our empathy for the physical pain suffered. The apostolic witnesses, seeing rather the appalling reality of the real death and the real ending of a real human life, write of the physical sufferings of the tortures preceding and accompanying the death of Jesus tersely, with little attention to any inventory of what the real sufferings must have been. Whatever is mentioned has symbolic significance or contributes to an understanding of the political implications of the execution.[22] The apostolic focus is on the death of Jesus as an event of such blinding revelation that his followers were not even able to see it for some time.

What is revealed in the death of Jesus is, of course, a profound mystery which cannot be adequately rendered in any verbal formulation and which cannot even be understood with great depth by one who is not yet dying. Nevertheless, the cumulative experience, prayer and reflection of the Church offers some approaches to the mystery. Jesus had made great promises to his followers, he had spoken with confidence about his own relation to the heavenly Father (and therefore by implication about his personal destiny), and he had given himself, his own life, as the pledge of his promises and of the truth of his vision of the hoped-for future. To his sinful followers then and now, his death (looked at without evasions) is in the first place appalling— the collapse of all the promises and all the hope. Looked at in the light of our ordinary criteria, his death can only be seen as a dismal failure of power to accomplish his purpose. If we are to trust the apostolic witness, what makes the difference in this bleak picture is the slowly dawning awareness that to him who suffered this "untimely" torture death it was not the failure of power to accomplish his purpose but rather a personal consummation of that power. With this realization, however improbable it may at first seem, it is the very death of Jesus

that becomes the pledge of his promises and of the vision of the hoped
for future.

Traditional piety at a very simple level has always grasped this
truth in some measure. The thought has been expressed that if Jesus
loves the human community so much that he radically surrenders himself to accomplish his purpose, then the love of God which is expressed
in his death is more compassionate than one might have dared to hope.
Then, moreover, the redemptive power of God reaches further into the
network of interdependent willful human freedoms than one might
have supposed it could (given the existence of created freedom). In
other words, traditional piety has looked at the death of Jesus, saying
in effect that God is other than we could ever have supposed God to
be by reading off the possibilities out of our own cumulative experience without Jesus. The death of Jesus reveals the peak of human
perfection in the one whose self-possession is sufficient to ground an
unreserved gift of himself. In him the perfection of human freedom is
revealed not as utmost independence but as total transcendence of
self-seeking, bursting barriers to human community in such a radical
way that universal possibilities erupt from it.

It is for these reasons that the symbol of the cross at the center
of Christianity is significant. We could have had at the center of
Christian memory, consciousness and iconography the figure of Jesus
teaching. Instead we have given the place of honor to the crucified and
dying Jesus. It is the image of a man bound and restrained, of a man
marginated from decision making and manipulative power, of a man
whose fate is thrust upon him. It could be the image of a man totally
unfree, totally dehumanized. That is certainly the initial shocking
impact that the image of the cross conveys. Only by entering into the
"mind and heart" of this man to try to fathom the meaning of his
death from within the dying of it does the believer transcend the scandal of the cross. Scandal is essentially in the cross. It is only the
unthinking familiarity with the cross as liturgical symbol that blunts
the edge of the impact, and such blunted perception is far from Christian faith. Faith really only begins where the shocking contradiction

of this symbol is felt and confronted. The sign of our salvation is the sign of the destruction of the human. It is not by evading this realization but by moving into it and through it that Christians can come to some sense of the liberating death of Jesus and what is revealed in it.

What we learn in Jesus is that to be human is to appropriate reality in order to give, to become in order to serve, to be so as to be for others, to live because the purpose of life is beyond oneself and to die because human existence is oriented to communion. What we experience in the death of Jesus is the power to realize the human—the creative divine power reaching redemptively down through the murkiest levels of inhumanity, radically transforming the possibilities of human freedom from within. The point here, however, is not first and foremost that Jesus is so different from everybody else, but rather that being "of one substance with us according to his manhood" he redeems and transforms our possibilities from within. This is the manner in which death may be said to "lose its sting." This also would seem to be an underlying motif in the extraordinary respect and attention that is given to the martyrs in the early Church, where eucharistic language and parallelism with the passion of Jesus are not uncommonly applied to the accounts of the deaths of the martyrs. They indeed are admired, in a sense even envied, for having entered into the liberating mystery of Christ in which death loses the sting of defeat and frustration and becomes instead a "birthday" into the fullness of being with the Lord in glory.

It is not only for the martyrs but for all Christians and for all human persons that the death of Jesus becomes a criterion by which other deaths are measured and judged, and through the deaths, of course, the persons who die. The death of Jesus becomes the mode of discernment of the degree of maturity of the human person. To die humanly is to complete the project of one's life and being as a self-gift. To die tragically or subhumanly is to succumb to biological death, still trying vainly to make oneself the end and purpose of one's own existence. What is characteristic of the death of Jesus is that the possibility of death as human act of fulfillment is realized in circumstances that most sharply incorporate the tension between the destructive and distintegrating aspect of death as the fate thrust upon the person and the constructive and integrating aspect of death as the consummation creatively willed by the person. The death of Jesus does not dissolve the paradox or tension, but rather grasps it radically and transcends it.

The apostolic community testifies to us that a great freedom erupted in their midst out of the death of Jesus and that they experienced the presence of Jesus after his death as no longer limited to one space, no longer restricted to the patterns of contact, communication and influence that characterize the biological lives of human beings. Moreover, they testify to us their certitude that this breakthrough is one that they will experience in their own deaths. This is an important connection in the vision and understanding of the early community of the followers of Jesus. It implies a continuity of experience and a certitude concerning their understanding of the outcome of the death of Jesus—a certitude that is directly rooted in their experience.

Reflection on the meaning of the death of Jesus can be severely impeded by a too facile understanding of the resurrection, which strips it of mystery and spiritual import and leaves it looking more like a magic trick. Unfortunately it is possible to present the death of Jesus as not really a death at all but a three-day sleep in the tomb of a divine person whose foreknowledge offered him a clear view of the whole course of events prior to the passion, and prior to his decision to suffer crucifixion. If such were the case, there would have been no death at all but simply the charade of going through a death. But on this matter Church teaching has been very clear: Jesus really suffered and really died.[23] Resurrection, then, cannot be seen simply as resumption of the same life, briefly interrupted, nor as resuscitation of a corpse after the irreversible symptoms of death had set in. The message of resurrection is one of a breakthrough that occurred in the person of one who did indeed die. The resurrection is presented to us by its primary witnesses as a transformation into a new mode of presence and communication.

The question that is important here is why and how the apostolic witnesses enjoyed such certitude about their own resurrection and that of all the members of the community. We could bypass the experiential questions by pointing out that the idea of resurrection was not new and was taken over with the existing pattern of expectations. In fact, the popular hope at the time of Jesus among Jews was that when the messianic era, the day of the Lord, the reign of the heavens, was realized, all the just and faithful of Israel who had died in expectation would be aroused from the sleep of their death and raised from the bed of the tomb to participate in the rejoicing. There is no doubt that when the apostolic community was groping for words to express the ineffable experience of the transformed presence of Jesus among them after his death, they gratefully took over this language and imagery of the bodily (personal) "getting up from the couch" of the tomb. Some scholars would even argue that the apostolic community used this language for the obvious reason that the tomb was in fact found inexplicably empty,[24] thus verifying the popular expectation. Yet this should not be pressed too far. The existing expectation was for an immediate consummation and public establishment or realization of the heavenly reign to which those who had died before it came would be summoned from their tombs. It was really a new and difficult realization that the messianic age, already initiated in the resurrection of Jesus, might take so long to come about in its fullness that all the original witnesses would be long dead. Indeed it seems at first to have been rather a scandal to the community that any followers of Jesus should die before the general fulfillment.

From the foregoing it would seem that the projected resurrection of the dead yet to come could not have been taken over unthinkingly from past expectations but springs from a conviction that is evidently rooted in the present experience of the community. That experience is not exactly one of empathy with the risen Jesus, for we receive no testimonies whatsoever concerning what the resurrection was like for

Jesus himself, that is, concerning what it was like to be the risen Jesus. The testimonies we have concern what it was like for others to encounter the risen Jesus. In other words, they are largely testimonies of the new life that had exploded in the community of his followers. That new life seems to be intimately connected with the experience that the presence of Jesus, which during his biological life had been a presence to them but outside them, became in the transformation of the resurrection a presence interior to themselves. His presence to them and his communion with them seemed to be no longer mediated by another, distinct body oppositional to their own, but seemed rather to come to them in a bodiliness that was inclusive of their own and of their whole environment. In any case, they are able to speak of having risen with Christ, even though they have not yet biologically died. They are able to claim in some sense to speak directly from their own experience as an experience within the resurrection even before death.

It is for this reason, no doubt, that contemporary thought has begun to emphasize present Christian experience as the source from which we are to know and understand what is intended in the doctrine of the resurrection of the dead.[25] We have all experienced new life and hope beyond tragedy and a new coming into being beyond painful and basic kinds of self-surrender. In a Christian community in which deep personal faith structures strong community mediation of the presence of Jesus, such experiences of rebirth and resurrection can be intense and very tangible to others. Characteristic of such rebirths is invariably the sense of a breaking of barriers to communion with God and others and with the world as a whole. One's life seems to be lived more in others. The obvious examples of this in daily Christian life of ordinary people are marriage and parenthood. These events in our lives may indeed find us closed and selfish and essentially unchanged, but wherever there is a death there is also some measure of transformation into more intense and less exclusive levels of being and experience. Really to love and share with even one other person involves surrender of individual goals and pursuits for common ones, surrender of self-constituting privacy for family-constituting intimacy. Family in any

true sense means a kind of surrender of one's private body; one's pre-
viously privately owned body becomes in a sense family property in
work, in procreation and in planning, while one's consciousness is no
longer encompassed in the experience of this one body but somehow
moves into the larger body of the family. The matter is underscored
in our culture for women who lose even their own names when they
marry.

All these experiences of surrender of control and surrender of
self-interest are, of course, experiences of the dimension of our lives
that is consummated in death. No matter how inadequately one
responds to the call for such continuous surrenders, the on-going experience of them gives us some understanding of what it is to die. Likewise, the transformed mode of being beyond each such surrender or
dying gives us the analogy by which to understand what is meant by
resurrection. Such an analogy is complemented and intensified by
whatever the community is able to mediate of the living presence and
power of Jesus in its midst in the present time and situation.

All of this does not give us a glimpse beyond death, in the sense
of factual information of what lies beyond. What this cumulative
experience does give us are reasonable grounds of credibility and solid
grounds of hope for a passage through death to heightened and intensified life. It also suggests as a model for thinking about and expressing
this hope, the image of human reflexive self-consciousness disengaging
itself from the limits of the individual body to become incorporated in
the larger dimensions of the community.

5
Beyond the Gates of Death

As pointed out in earlier chapters, Christian eschatology does nothing to satisfy curiosity concerning what lies beyond death. The question may well be raised, therefore, as to why there should be any teaching about it at all. The Church might, for instance, simply teach that our responsibility is to work for the redemption of the world within history and that our personal, individual destiny is in God's hands. Or the Church teaching might end with the observation that in death we fall asleep in the Lord. However, when one begins to imagine alternate ways of approaching the questions about what is beyond death, two points emerge clearly. First of all, it becomes clear that there is no way of speaking about it without metaphors such as "falling asleep" and "in God's hands." In other words, to escape from the language of poetry and very concrete symbols is impossible in this matter. Secondly, it soon becomes clear that we are not satisfied with an answer that rephrases the question without somehow formulating Christian hope of individual salvation and fulfillment.

Moreover, it is not at all a matter of indifference which symbols and images are used to express our hope. This, no doubt, is the reason for the concern of the Church *magisterium* over the centuries to "guard against error" in a matter in which we are necessarily using figurative language. As mentioned in Chapter 3, there has been consistent stress laid on the seriousness and the finality of the outcome of a human life at death.[26] Any suggestion that there is not really such a thing as hell, or that it is not "eternal," has been vigorously rejected in the official Church teaching. This could be read as a fundamentalist preoccupation to preserve the literal meaning of the symbol as though it had a one-to-one correspondence with the reality. But there seems to be something at stake that is more serious and certainly more spiritually significant. Given that we must think and express ourselves in analogies when we speak of what is beyond death, given that fire is a particularly striking symbol as pointed out in Chapter 3, and given that we can only speak in temporal dimensions on the analogy of our actual experience, what is central in the statement is the insistence on ultimate accountability for what we do with our lives. It is not claimed that the picture of one burning in everlasting flames bears a one-to-one correspondence with the outcome of anyone's life. In fact, it has never been officially taught that any human persons were or would be "in hell." The insistence was on hell as a possibility. It is the possibility that speaks clearly of the seriousness of the human task or calling. Further, to describe hell as immediate after death and as eternal is simply to underscore the above by insisting on the finality of death. Any representation that would imply the possibility of simple oblivion, or of a "general judgment" in which the individual remains anonymous in the outcome for the world, would suggest something far less exigent and far less ineluctably urgent.

Similarly significant is the concern with bodily resurrection. Actually, as our Christian theology shaped itself into explanations in the categories of Greek philosophy, there is no doubt that it would have simplified matters in the explanations if we had dropped or explained away the doctrine of resurrection in favor of a simple doctrine of the natural immortality of the soul, enhanced by the proclamation of a graced (supernatural) destiny of more intimate union with God than is implicit in the claim of natural immortality. It is certainly in many ways a more credible image to hold before the believer. Our own introspective sense of the indestructibility of our reflexive self-awareness has been very strong in the West until quite recently when the biological emphasis in experimental psychology has influenced self-perception. Given this cultural image of the human person as an incorporated soul that must have somewhere to go after the "death of the body," the continued insistence on the rising again (or getting up from sleep) of the body calls for special attention. This is accentuated by the fact that the Church did take over the Greek understanding of the immortality of the soul and yet, somewhat inconsistently, taught bodily resurrection alongside it. In the course of this teaching, death became defined as the separation of body and soul, so that resurrection is imaged as the reclamation of a material body by the continually surviving soul.

This set of images and representations has in fact led to some very awkward questions, such as the question as to where the souls reside in the interval when not "in the body." On close analysis most of these questions turn out to be non-questions, because they only make sense while one makes the assumption that the images in which Christian hope is expressed are to be taken as literally intended. As soon as it is realized that these images are poetic projections and in no way satisfy curiosity or intend to inform about after death, it also becomes clear that the real questions to be asked are of a different order. Here the real question seems to be: What understanding is it that is being safeguarded by the insistence of the image of the arising of the body? The use of this image is a way of insisting, in spite of everything else that is being said, that the human person is not an incorporated soul but a living body whose life is spiritual. The body is not an outer shell to be husked off and discarded when the inner kernel, the soul, is ripe. Rather the body is the expression of personal existence. It gives that existence its actual dimensions, and particularly its relational possibilities.

To express Christian hope in bodily terms is to imply something about the way our present life is to be evaluated. It implies that the dimensions of our lives that have ultimate importance are not limited to inner consciousness and prayer and withdrawal from common life and social intercourse and responsibility. Rather it suggests that the social dimensions of our lives have ultimate importance. It means that the need for physical, emotional and cultural sustenance is not to be despised and set aside as irrelevant—most especially not when it is the need of others for sustenance that is at stake. In fact, the whole emphasis on resurrection seems rather to suggest that the spiritual is not what is opposed to the bodily but what is opposed to the self-centered and selfish, no matter how intellectual or immaterial the selfish interests may be.

Another aspect of the doctrine of resurrection that tends to confirm this is the social context in which it is presented in its original Jewish setting.[27] The teaching of the inter-testamental period, which is taken over in the preaching of Jesus and in the proclamation of the resurrection of Jesus by the apostolic community, referred to participation in the general rejoicing when God vindicates his faithful ones, fulfilling his promises. It implied an image of being ushered into a feast, participating in a community celebration. What seems to be implied in this is the maturation of relationships and bonds of communion. Such bonds cannot, of course, be suddenly created without the inner, free, self-transformation of the persons involved, from self-centeredness to a focus on others. Such a self-transformation can only be a life project shaping and determining the whole process of becoming of the person. In other words, it could in no way be seen as an arbitrary reward, and therefore cannot be isolated from the ordering of values and priorities during one's biological life. This must have been clearly recognized by the apostolic community as witnessed by the inclusion in the Gospels of such passages as Matthew 25. This text and others like it really do not allow of any vision of future happiness to be attained by withdrawing from the world and its problems to a life of contemplation and preoccupation with personal avoidance of sin and personal attainment of salvation.

At the same time there is some ambiguity in the images of resurrection. As in the case of the resurrection of Jesus, so in the expectation of the general resurrection, there lurks some danger of misinterpretation. It might be falsely supposed that because of the hope of resurrection death is no more than a door or archway or tunnel which hides what is at the other side but simply interrupts a life that continues essentially unchanged. It is a danger of misinterpretation with which much contemporary thought has been deeply concerned.[28] If the life beyond is more or less a continuation, then death loses some of the ultimate exigence that it places on human lives. If we do not know what to expect beyond death in any factual way, death places the absolute exigence to make sense of the life that we do know within the dimensions and terms of that life as we know it. In other words, there can be no childish hope for more or less magical solutions of personal and interpersonal problems.

This, of course, has been stressed in Church teaching in the emphasis on the possibility of damnation and the finality of the choices made at the time of death. It has been taught explicitly that there is no repentance beyond death. But the subtle and many-dimensional unfolding of a person involves so much more than a choice for or against grave sin. It involves the appropriation of one's whole being in its aspects of facticity and its aspects of freedom. It involves, for instance, the appropriation of one's sexuality (in the broadest sense of that word) in a world whose sinful history sets up sex role definitions that are elaborately inauthentic. Likewise, it involves full appropriation of one's adult personhood with the inherent responsibilities, in a world whose patterns of greed and domination tend to convey the sense that most human persons are called upon only to mark time in history, uncritically and uncreatively filling the slots into which economic necessity has channeled them, without any responsibility for the justice and humaneness of the structures of society.

One might give many specific examples of the foregoing. The important point at issue is that any understanding of death and resurrection which implies a simple resumption of an unfinished life can far too easily ground an image of the whole of human life as the "antechamber" where one must keep the rules and wait patiently to be allowed to pass through the door into the other part of one's life—the "part that counts." The difficulty is precisely that there is a reduction of the whole of life to a "part that does not really count" except to pass a qualifying examination for living the "real part." To insist on the reality and finality of death, as the Church has certainly done in its teachings on hell, is to insist that there is no human maturing, no "growing up" from childishness or half-conscious living into adulthood after death. The image of God in which the human person is created is something to be achieved in the course of biological life or not at all. The possibilities of awakening to full consciousness and full self-consciousness and full human responsibility happens during the biological life span or not at all. This involves far more than staying out of trouble, keeping rules, or "being good" in the sense in which this last is usually understood. What is required is the appropriation of one's own process of becoming and of one's community process of becoming in a way that involves far more adult maturity and far more acceptance of responsibility and risk than most people are taught to aspire to grasp.

This is certainly a serious challenge to each of us in our attitudes to our own deaths. The issue is even more fraught with consequences, as the "liberation theology" of Latin America has been pointing out in our times,[29] when we are defining, explicitly or implicity, the salvation of others and the relationship between their biological lives and their personal destiny. Any understanding of death, judgment, resurrection, heaven, hell and purgatory, which envisions salvation beyond death for people in flat contradiction of the stunted state of human development and human consciousness that is expected of them in their biological lives, is clearly a magical understanding. It is an understanding that wishes death away into something less final, less real, less consequential. It is an understanding that wishes the true personhood of the others away out of this life where it might disturb our privilege or our greed into the realm beyond death where we expect some unspecified multiplication of possibilities without social or community limitations. By the same token it is an understanding that sees a salvation beyond death that somehow bypasses the real becoming of the real person in real interpersonal relationships and personal responsibility and self-awareness.

This ambiguity of the imagery appears also in the important area of the projection of "heaven." The literal meaning of heaven as "the sky," the place "up there," the ethereal other place, is not at issue here, and does not seem to pose a serious contemporary problem. The ambiguity that seems to endanger Christian hope lies in the shift from the "reign of the heavens" within the human community to the "beatific vision." Clearly it is a shift from a certain earthly Hebrew concreteness to a more speculative Greek remoteness. It is also a shift from a communal to an individualist image. The advantage of the imagery of the "beatific vision" (the looking that makes happy) is, of course, that it pinpoints the core of human fulfillment as the relationship with God. In this sense it certainly suggests a continuity between the way a human life is oriented in its total process of becoming and the final or definitive outcome. It suggests that the essential element of a good life is that it is prayerful, contemplative, "tuning in" to the call that brings it into being, and listening with obedient readiness. It suggests the deep realization and acceptance of creatureliness in an attitude of gratitude and adoration. All this is certainly in harmony with the Gospel of salvation in Jesus Christ. In fact, it even describes very closely the quality of Jesus' own life as presented in the Gospels.

The disadvantage of the imagery of the "beatific vision" is in its one-sided presentation of the human person and the relation of the human person to God. The image of looking, of contemplation, strongly suggests that the reality of the human person is somehow contained in an isolated consciousness. Although Christian teaching has long rejected the anthropology of the Gnostic movements, there is a certain nostalgic remnant of Gnosticism in Christian piety that expresses itself in eschatology and correspondingly in Christian asceticism. If the goal of human striving is rightly portrayed as an individual contemplation of God, seen directly without mediation of the rest of creation, then a good life is only accidentally concerned with relationships with others and responsibility for others. But this type of attitude and understanding is very clearly inconsistent with the Gospel, which makes charity the core of spirituality and presents the love of God and neighbor as mutually dependent and inseparable. Observation bears this out in practice. It is possible to live a colossally selfish and self-centered life while preoccupied with attaining mystical contemplation and saving one's soul. When charity is taken seriously as the criterion of the good life, then it is clear that it is not the earthiness and concreteness of one's concerns that turns one away from God, but rather the self-centeredness of concerns no matter how lofty and aerial. Likewise, it may be said, it is not even the conflictual and absorbing nature of one's concerns that would lead one to "tune out" the divine call and exigence, but rather the self-serving, self-aggrandizing element of any activity no matter how serene and sublime. Yet a model of heaven which places the emphasis on solitary serenity of intimacy with God in contemplation creates the hazard of a self-centered way of judging the concrete reality of the life between birth and death which we know and for which we must accept full responsibility.

It would seem that the Hebrew symbol of the "reign of the heavens" (where heaven is, of course, a circumlocution for God) is a better balanced expression of Christian hope. Rightly understood, it implies an intimate knowing of God, even a tender relationship, which is nevertheless not separated from the concrete reality of daily living and actual human existence in its multiple relationships, its physical experience and its context in nature and history. Likewise it implies no contradiction between the stance of "tuning in" to God in ultimate obedient readiness and the absorbing concern to build a good world in the political, economic and cultural dimensions of public life. Concern for the human community as a whole need not then be seen as basically antithetical to concern for the salvation of one's own soul. Rather they are seen as identical because one saves one's own soul by giving one's life in concern for others. The quest of the reign of the heavens need not and should not be seen as excluding the prayerful and contemplative dimension of life. The goal is the gift of God, but it is a gift that can only be received "according to the mode of the receiver," and that is a social, communitarian, actively responsible mode of concern for others and for the community as a whole.

This is no doubt the reason for the contemporary tendency of theologians to focus on general rather than individual eschatology. There has been an awakening to the danger of a presentation of images of Christian hope that may inspire selfishness rather than charity, focus on self rather than surrender of self, refusal to die rather than the transcending of the tragedy of death, and therefore ultimately the losing of life rather than its saving. The reestablishment of hope for the redemption of the world at the center of consciousness does not imply a lack of concern with hope for the individual, but it does transform the quest for individual salvation in terms of the primacy of charity.

It is for these reasons also that images of Christian hope based on the vision of Teilhard de Chardin seem gradually to be gaining ground.[30] In the evolutionary view of Teilhard, when evolution becomes conscious of itself in the human community the challenge becomes that of community. The creative selflessness of Jesus appears within human history as the point toward which all things and persons are destined to move. The maturity and fulfillment of the process of becoming of the human individual, the human race as a whole, and even the universe as a whole, then appears as movement toward community and harmony at the deepest levels of being. This understanding has inspired a way of imaging the destiny of the human person after or beyond death in which the reflexive self-consciousness that has been rooted in the single, discrete organism of one human body extends its base and becomes rooted in the totality of the community and the cosmos.

This kind of imagery has the advantage of suggesting an essential continuity between the vocation of charity and the outcome. It has the disadvantage that it is not yet formulated in an analogy clear enough and familiar enough to make much sense to most believers. The biblical imagery of the reign of God, the heavenly celebration, the wedding feast, still seems to be stronger.

6
Salvation Now and Later

The earliest community of the followers of Jesus proclaimed that Jesus was risen and they were his witnesses because they were already risen with him and were awaiting the fulfillment of his transformed presence among them. The hope that moved them was hope for the full actualizing of this presence of Jesus in the human community through its extension to more people and through its intensification in the lives of those who had already been touched. These early followers of Jesus looked to the fulfillment of what had begun within their own experience. Certainly we have evidence from the letters of Paul that some speculation about the hoped-for future resurrection had already begun within New Testament times, but speculation about life beyond death and its qualities and conditions was not typical of this earliest Christian period. Preoccupation with such speculation seems to become stronger as there is less experiential base for it in a transformed present way of life.

Much of the contemporary reflection on individual eschatology has been concerned precisely to re-establish the earlier connection.[31] The pertinent choice is not the choice between salvation now or salvation later, but the choice of salvation in charity now and later or perdition in selfishness now and later. Christians have often too lightly caricatured Judaism as being concerned with this-worldly salvation now rather than spiritual salvation "in the next world." Likewise they have been quick to reject Marxist and socialist thought out of hand and in its entirety on the assumption that concern with the happiness of human persons within their biological lifetimes and within their total human context must be antithetical to any concern for spiritual salvation. At root, this perception of two mutually exclusive categories is, of course, Gnostic rather than Christian, as has been pointed out in previous chapters. It implies the existence of two creating principles that are hostile to each other. It interprets the tension between matter and spirit, which we undeniably all experience, as essential and insoluble in human existence rather than as an accident of sinful history ultimately redeemable by the one God who creates the totality of a good world.

In the biblical context of our Christian origins, just as there is not a dual and necessarily conflictual creation of good spirit and bad matter, so there cannot be a conflict between this-worldly and other-worldly salvation. Salvation of the person, the real person and the whole person that exists concretely, can only be salvation now and later—it cannot coherently be understood as either salvation now or later. This follows directly from the unity of creation by the one God and from the claim that salvation is by charity. Catholic teaching has, in fact, insisted on the intrinsic connection between charity and grace and salvation: grace is the present relationship or communion with God that blossoms or unfolds into salvation, and charity is that quality of action which, seen as a disposition of being, is also called grace. If we take this seriously, it has far-reaching consequences for an understanding of the quest for salvation. It implies a qualitative continuity between personal development throughout life and its fulfillment in the ultimate destiny of the person.

It is basic in the Christian understanding that what we need to be saved or redeemed from is sin and selfishness and consequent unhappiness and personal lack of focus and purpose in our existence. What we need to be redeemed for is personal happiness and focus in the integration of our whole being in response to God who calls us to communion with him. These are central and standard themes of

Christian teaching but contemporary experience and awareness have given a new edge to them.

One realization that our society has come to is the awareness of how intimately courage, energy, zest for life and willingness to undertake arduous endeavors are all bound up with physical health and well-being. Ecological and nutritional studies have made us aware of it, particularly in what has been observed in situations of extensive and systematic malnutrition or environmental damage to health. Practitioners of yoga and similar disciplines have also drawn attention to it by demonstrating the difference made in a human life by a regular and balanced routine of consumption and rest and activity. In fact, it is a noticeable phenomenon in our society today that many people who turn away from Christianity as an irrelevant quest for salvation that does not make sense to them will make a radical commitment to a quest for salvation along practical lines that seem to have more connection with the real life that they know. In the practice of yoga or transcendental meditation or similar disciplines they claim to have found some analogue of what the early followers of Jesus said they had found—the experiential beginning of salvation. They claim that they can experience themselves coming to wholeness or integration and being able to appropriate their own being more coherently and creatively.

Although this kind of experience of salvation certainly falls short of the Christian goal of salvation by charity, it indicates something important about the becoming of the human person that cannot really be bypassed. It is not possible to give what one has not got. One cannot really give oneself to others in loving concern and service when one does not have a certain minimum degree of self-possession. Except in persons who are already very mature and integrated human beings, intense anxiety, constant hunger, deprivation, pain, frustration and humiliation all militate fiercely against the basic integration and self-possession from which a self-gift to others can be made. Equally hostile to such self-possession, however, is a life of pampered self-indulgence in which the physiological base for a focused and integrated life is missing for want of disciplined personal habits.

Neither those who lack the basic necessities of physical life and health nor those who squander them because they lack self-discipline are really well placed to allow their lives and being to be transformed by charity (grace). This realization has overwhelmed us in our own times, mainly from non-Christian sources. Yet it corresponds to the earliest Christian notions of asccticism which were characterized by simplicity of life and community sharing of resources. What it implies for the continuity of salvation in this life and ultimately is that there is need for a constant creative restructuring of human society by those ideals of simplicity of life and community sharing of resources.

Running parallel to this realization of the fundamental importance of physiological health and well-being is the growing realization of the importance of personal security. Anyone who is constantly preoccupied with self-defense is not open for compassion and common concerns. Personal security is based on positive experiences of having one's basic needs filled. To speak airily of eternal salvation in relation to people who live their whole lives under threat of starvation, or in imminent danger of death from violence or disease or natural disasters, is irresponsible. It is the immediate need of salvation from the immediate terror that must first be confronted, because the ultimate fulfillment of the human person simply does not bypass the concrete needs. It has long been axiomatic among Christian foreign missionaries that it is pointless to preach the Gospel to people with empty stomachs. This is true, of course, in the first place because preaching a Gospel of love without practicing it suggests that the preacher does not really believe in it himself. But there is an even more urgent reason for the unutility of the enterprise. There is an order of priorities in human attention and focus. Human attention and effort is drawn not necessarily to what is most important but rather to what is most urgent. Personal physical survival is always most urgent unless and until a person has reached that degree of personal integration and maturity at which one is truly ready to sacrifice oneself for others. But this is precisely the kind of human maturity and integration that must be attained by the growth and becoming of the whole person which rests on the personal security based on fulfillment of basic needs.

Here again, the realization comes to us overwhelmingly out of the contemporary awareness of the dynamics and constellation of human personality that we draw from contemporary secular sources. Yet it is by no means hostile or even strange to the classic patterns of Christian spirituality. That the Christian community should be a kind of insurance against misfortune and want for its members, that it should be concerned with making peace and with reconstructing within its own ranks a just and dependable order is a classic Christian understanding. That in the modern world this involves worldwide concerns with peace and justice, with the guarantee of a living wage, of fair dealings with poor and powerless countries and special protection for minorities and powerless groups—all this has been the theme of the modern papal social encyclical letters and of conciliar and synodal statements.

In basic personal security there also lies a complementarity. Our contemporary knowledge of social, economic and political interaction forces us to acknowledge that the insecurity of the poor becomes in short order the insecurity of the rich, simply because there comes a point of desperation that precipitates violent despoliation or furtive sabotage or plain theft. Likewise the insecurity of the powerless can in short order become the insecurity of the powerful by way of assassinations and guerrilla warfare. What we have learned of epidemics has extended this into the health field. What we are beginning to learn about food and population seems to extend the principle of common security and insecurity to basic survival. Inflationary patterns suggest something similar within a national economy. From all these aspects it is clear that personal security is a community project and that there can be no foundation of personal security for human growth to maturity unless there is constant concern with building up structures in society that favor security by restraining greed and lust for power.

Not less important than personal security is a positive and comfortable self-identity. One of the most common ways that privileged people in our society seek for personal salvation is by psychiatric care and counseling, psychoanalysis, group therapy and so on. The non-privileged of the society who could not afford such expensive quests for wholeness and identity often seek a similar effect by aligning themselves with minority power groups. What people feel to be an urgent priority in deploying their time and resources and energies usually turns out to be foundational in personal growth, and therefore foundational also in growth in charity or the ability and disposition to be for others and for God. Certainly, contemporary experience and observation tends to suggest that love and generosity do not readily come from people with a negative, shame-plagued self-image. Such people are more likely to be furtively undercutting or shamelessly bullying others, to be playing destructive games of one-upmanship, to be closed to the needs of others and officious in positions of public trust, to be suspicious and easily offended, to be sadistic toward those more vulnerable than themselves, to sabotage community efforts and relationships, to intervene to destroy trust between others, and in many ways to further the history of sin rather than the history of redemption. One does not need to be a practicing psychiatrist or psychologist to know this; quiet observation in any business, school, political structure or neighborhood or voluntary association soon illustrates the point.

It is clear that a person or society that behaves predominantly in these destructive ways is not growing in charity or grace or moving toward final salvation. Yet those who do so, insecure people with a negative self-image, cannot really rescue themselves out of this pattern. One can, of course, pray that they be redeemed out of it, but the ordinary answer to that prayer would be community action that builds and restores their self-esteem. The Christian community from the beginning has been concerned with this, with the elimination of hurtful discriminations, of class and racial boundaries and other patterns of exclusivity that would give rise to what we would recognize today as the self-devaluation that tends to be part of minority group consciousness. It is the business of community, and in a special way of any community claiming to be Christian, to give its members the foundation of a positive self-image on which any call to service of the community and of others can be based.

To say that a minimum of physical well-being, a basic personal security and a positive image are foundational to becoming a person in the full sense is certainly to say that they are foundational to charity, grace and salvation. It is certainly not to say that they are to be equated with these. The person, in a Christian perspective, is not saved when these needs are met, but only when this has served as a basis for full appropriation of one's life in order to make a gift of it to others and ultimately to God. Because this project is never complete until one's whole life has been lived and one's death died, salvation clearly is not complete this side of death. Yet this does not imply a qualitative difference such as would put salvation outside present experience categorically and on principle. It is rather the opposite that is true; if salvation is ecstatic union with God, then there ought to be progressive experience of salvation in the life of an individual and of a Christian community. As one's life becomes less self-centered and selfish and more a gift to others and an offering of praise and thanksgiving to God, there should indeed normally be a growing peace and serenity and the kind of joy that comes of personal integration and purposefulness. The lives of the saints that we have canonized do in fact constantly testify to such progressive redemption or salvation of the person, and one may assume that it is of this that the earliest followers of Jesus speak when they claim already to have risen with Christ.

If the foregoing is taken seriously, however, there is continuity not only in salvation now and ultimately, but also between personal salvation of the individual and the redemption of the whole society by the reclaiming and reshaping of its sinful structures at every level. The community which we are is called on to be the living presence of the risen Christ—to be his body in the Pauline language, mediating the saving grace of God by the upbuilding of individuals and of structures. In any community the persons who compose it are at various stages of growth and maturity. The gift of those who are more mature meets the basic need of those who need yet to find some support for fuller self-appropriation before they will be ready to be in any sense of the word generous in a self-gift to others. We are all accustomed to fulfilling this supportive role as parents of young children, without resentment or surprise. There is not always an equal willingness to play such a role remedially or redemptively for people who are adult in years but incapacitated for love because they lack the personal foundations.

It is at this point that growth in charity and grace toward the fullness of salvation ceases to be a bland and almost automatic process in the society. The sign of the cross of Christ is upon the endeavor because the immature and incapacitated people frequently have great political, economic and social power to hurt and destroy and perpetuate among others their own patterns of inadequacy. It is in this way, after all, that we have a history of sin which calls for a history of redemption, a drama of the broken Adam in scattered fragments that calls for the new man, Christ, as principle of reintegration. But a history of sin, reinforced by vested interests, by structural deposits and accumulations and by fear and insecurities, makes for a deeply conflictual world. This in turn makes the whole process of salvation a painful one that calls for an heroic counterculture stance more often than not. It also calls for a strong community stance and community action if anything is to be gained. Such a conflictual context is always in flux. It is not dealt with by a dogged following of rules. It can only be dealt with by great creativity and spontaneity. But this will only be forthcoming if there is a basis for discernment in personal experience, that is, if salvation is something of which one has already had a foretaste so that one knows the salvific action or response by its own intrinsic quality. The testimony of the earliest generations seems to suggest that this is ordinarily the heritage of the Christian community as a whole and not only of a few gifted or privileged individuals within it.

Obviously such continuous discernment in ever changing situations is not made lightly. The whole Christian tradition seems to insist on the necessary grounding of it in community worship and a certain existential depth of personal prayer. It is equally grounded in an on-

going openness to personal conversion in charity, because one does not
find answers without asking the right questions, and one does not ask
the right questions if one is not willing to take the risks inherent in
those questions. But there seems to be a third element that is necessary
to provide the basis for such continuous discernment, and that is the
receptivity and support of a community that encourages, collaborates
and evaluates.

Contemporary eschatology tends to emphasize human initiative
and creativity more than has perhaps been done for many centuries.
For this reason, the objection is sometimes posed, to any discussion
such as the foregoing, that salvation is after all, when all is said and
done, the work and gift of God, so that it is rather the divine initiative
and creativity that ought to be stressed in any account of Christian
hope. The difficulty in answering this question lies in the assumption
on which it is based, namely, that divine initiative and human initiative are opposed to each other as distinct and mutually exclusive categories which are perhaps even hostile to each other. If this were so,
then the human condition for salvation might be the greatest possible
passivity and the foregoing of all initiative. However, contemporary
eschatology rests squarely on the assumption that divine initiative is
exercised in the world and its history primarily in the empowerment
and summoning forth of human freedom and creativity. In this case
the human condition for salvation is the greatest possible creativity
remaining as sensitively alert as possible to the Spirit of God which
Christians know as the Spirit of Jesus.

Conclusion

All of the foregoing leaves some practical questions unanswered. It leaves questions about what to say to the dying and to the bereaved. It leaves questions about one's own facing of death, and it leaves questions about the traditional Catholic devotions in which saints are not only honored and remembered but are addressed in prayer.

The early followers of Jesus recorded the attitudes of Jesus himself to similar questions in his own times. In the issue over resurrection between Pharisees and Sadducees there is no doubt that he sides with the Pharisees. When he answers the quaint dilemma over conflicting claims posed to him by the Sadducees (Mt. 22:23-33), Jesus rejects any literal interpretation of the imagery used. He insists that the reality eludes our imagining and all our calculations and inferences. At the same time he insists on the importance of the imagery and will not allow it to be argued away. It is important to express hope, and it must be expressed in the projections that are available.

A similar instance occurs in the letters of Paul (1 Cor. 15). In response to some idle speculation about the nature of the risen body. Paul will only reiterate that it is all beyond imagining, that we do not know concretely the object of our hope and that any speculation that would try to overcome this gap can simply serve no good purpose. The image that Paul uses is a telling one. People sow seed in the ground, not in the hope that seed will rise but in the hope that something transformed and far greater will rise from the ground, namely the whole plant. It is an important image, and it occurs in the sayings of Jesus also. The image of the seed that truly dies in the transformation to a new life is an apt symbol for a human life surrendered in death.

In subsequent ages, as has been pointed out in earlier chapters, the image of resurrection was retained by the Church even when it did not seem to fit so neatly into the contemporary patterns of understanding, and the image of the great celebration does not cease to be pertinent. It would seem that the classic symbols do not lose their vigor or their relevance, though more and more believers come to a point where they are forced by their own understanding to ask some critical questions about the meaning of the classic symbols. It is a case in which there has to be a progression from a naive to a post-critical appropriation of the same symbol. When our contemporary understanding of reality leads to the question "Is it true?" the appropriate answer is neither yes nor no. The appropriate answer is to look again at what truth might mean in this context. And on that basis one can only conclude that it is the best way we have to express a reality that we cannot know concretely until we experience it.

When one considers what to say to the dying, the important factor is really not the way the symbols are explained in words. The really important factor is in the analogies in life experiences by which the dying person can apprehend the images of our faith and hope. Any true pastoral effort must begin with the expectations and apprehensions which this individual's experiences have built up. The task will certainly be easier in a community that lives by a vivid faith and hope—a community in which life beyond death is already experienced as among the earliest followers of Jesus, who claimed to share in his resurrection before they themselves had died. A vital community of faith mediates an almost tangible presence of God and therefore an almost tangible pledge of consummating union with God.

Experiences of hope beyond despair and of life beyond death happen, of course, in all situations in which there is an experience of loss—whatever the object of the loss may be. But the most crucial experience is that of the loss of another person in death. When a person comes to die, certainly one of the most important ways that death has been "rehearsed" and analogies have been established for facing death and interpreting the symbols of hope is by the experience of the deaths of others in the community. A community that is not afraid to gather around its dying and to be fully present to the bereaved, helping them to reconstitute their lives, is by that very fact building up the analogies by which the symbols of hope can be apprehended.

When one considers what to say to the bereaved, the situation is similar. The ways in which the symbols of faith and hope are explained in words are certainly much less significant that the real-life experiential base for understanding those symbols. This, of course, is why the more concrete and vivid symbols have a more lasting relevance. The mourner's real question is concerned with the relationship, the communion with those who have died. It is the presence of the dead that is missed and mourned, both their presence to us and our presence to them. This involves both the comfort of a comfortable presence and the challenge of an unfinished relationship. Often the mourner longs not only for the accustomed communion with the one now dead but also for the opportunity to redress a wrong, complete a service, or fulfill or redeem the relationship.

This is one of the needs and questions which the Church has long addressed in the doctrine of the "communion of saints." In relation to the deaths of others, as in relation to one's own death, the Church has been unwilling to obscure the radical finality of death as the end of the personal life project. Yet it has, in its official teachings, been equally unwilling to represent the dead as out of communion with the living and beyond the responsibility of the living. Hence the officially endorsed and liturgically incorporated prayers for the dead. To pray for the "souls in purgatory" is to lend one's personal concern and vital energies in some way to the completion of the essential life-commitment of the dead. It may, in particular cases, even be the concrete fulfillment of this through the change it makes in the living. In any case, prayer for the dead expresses very concretely the paradox of our relationship with them.

Prayer for the dead speaks much more to mourners than explanations of death or of the images of hope beyond death. Prayer for the dead reaches into the unknown mystery with hope, instead of meandering inconclusively around it. The message of the paradoxical continuity in discontinuity is best understood in the context of long experience of praying for the dead. In the actual practice of praying for the dead, one comes to realize that it does not bring them back to the biological life they have left behind, nor does it re-establish the mode of presence belonging to biological life, which must be totally surrendered. At the same time, in the practice of praying for the dead one comes to realize that one can resume life without that presence with renewed strength and experience a great healing. It is this experience that provides the analogy by which one can realize and accept in trust that beyond death there is healing and renewal also, though it is closed to our observation.

Every parting and absence of friends and family members in the course of life is in some measure a rehearsal for the great absence and parting of death. The manner in which all the absences and partings are experienced also influences the possibility of hope beyond death. It is true that to some extent each individual must face such experiences as an individual and learn to cope with them and grow to maturity through them. Yet it is also true that the presence or absence of the community to its members at times of loneliness and parting is an important factor that influences the individual's capacity for growing to maturity through such experiences. A Christian community that abandons to loneliness not only its widows and its elderly, but also and more particularly its divorced and separated members, may be failing in the work of faith, hope and charity more extensively than at first appears. There may be steps missing in the building up of the experience of being risen with Christ, not only for the individuals concerned but for the community as a whole.

What has been said of the custom of praying for the dead can in large measure also be said of the custom of praying to the saints, asking their intercession with God. This practice could, of course, be interpreted minimally as an acknowledgement, in the form of a request, of what the saints have already done with their lives—which certainly amounts to intercession on behalf of all in need of redemption. However, this minimalist statement does not accord with the real thrust of the message of the resurrection as discussed in Chapter 4. The preaching of the resurrection of Jesus arose out of the community's experience of his presence and power among them after his death, a transformed and enhanced presence that had become interior to them. As the expectation of the resurrection of the dead is based on the resurrection of Jesus as exemplar, it certainly implies the anticipation of enhanced presence and power within the community. Thus prayer for the intercession of the saints is as valid as prayer to the risen Jesus, because these rest on a common foundation.

If prayer for the intercession of the saints is taken seriously, as suggested here, it also is a reaching into the unknown mystery, as is the prayer on behalf of the dead. It sets up channels of communication and communion which are in no way dependent on our understanding of them in systematic or rational terms, or on our being able to "decode" the symbols. In prayer, the images and symbols stand intact and therefore are valid whatever they may "stand for" in a rational analysis. In fact what we know is that there can be no rational analysis that goes "behind the images" to the reality in this matter; there can only be reformulations of our projected hope that are more or less appropriate in the attitudes, values and objectives they support in our present. Hence the Church's concern with the concrete representations as embodying orthodoxy.

The really important and pastorally urgent question here is how we are going to protect the integrity of our symbols in a post-critical consciousness. To put this another way, the question is how to allow believers the possibility of taking the symbols of hope seriously and living by their light after these same believers have been driven by their modern consciousness to realize that the symbols are not to be taken in their immediate literal sense, but stand for much more. Once the individual believer has come to the realization that the symbols cannot be taken literally as representing the reality simply as it is, the temptation is explicitly or implicitly to discount the significance of the images altogether. The only way that most individuals will avoid this is by an explicit and helpful continuing use of the images in community life and worship, because most individual believers are not apt by temperament and training to find their way to creative solutions by their own individual initiative. Community life and worship, however, thrive on classic forms and imagery, and then in turn reinforce the functional meaning of these classic forms and images for participant individuals even in their private lives and prayers. It would seem presently to be very urgent in our culture to affirm and reiterate the doctrines of the resurrection of the dead and the communion of saints in prayerful settings where they need not be explained (or explained away) but can have a direct impact in the shaping of contemporary Christian awareness according to their own literary genre.

The crucial test of any understanding of individual eschatology is, of course, in the way in which it makes it possible to confront one's own death. It is only at this point that the underlying issue in the doctrinal paradoxes really becomes clear. The New Testament and traditional Church teachings emphasize the certainty of hope beyond death and despair on the one hand, but insist on leaving the content of the promises in figurative imagery on the other hand. The hope is important, but the content of the hope cannot be systematically deciphered—this is what the Church teaching appears in the last analysis to say. In terms of confronting one's own death, this means that a Christian death must ultimately be an act of utter trust and self-surrender. If salvation is by charity, then death demands that charity be mature in the person to the point of a total, unreserved gift of self. An unreserved gift of self implies that no control or security is retained, and this is death. This is real death, not a momentary interruption of a life known to continue more or less in the same continuous stream of consciousness as happens after sleep.

In facing one's own death, one finds a rather clear distinction between three possible attitudes in dying. First, there is the attitude that death is a biological necessity and that no further sense can be made of it. What might lie beyond cannot possibly be known, but it would be reasonable to suppose that, in terms of the individual reflexive self-awareness, nothing lies beyond. Moreover, it would then be reasonable not to lament the fact but to be reconciled to it as a necessity which it would be childish to contest or resist. One should simply put one's affairs in order, take leave of family and friends and slip out of existence, making as little fuss about it as possible, leaving happy memories and an honestly earned reputation with those who remain alive. That is necessarily the death of the good atheist or agnostic who has no personal God to whom to give praise or thanks, to whom to surrender one's life and being. It is by no means an ignoble death. It is in its own way profoundly unselfish, being a final act of courteous consideration of others. Inasmuch as it is a death that expresses considerable charity for others, it must certainly be in some high degree salvific. It is, perhaps, also quite extraordinary that anyone should die in this disposition.

At the opposite extreme to this attitude is the one that denies death in the name of religious faith. There is an attitude of hide-and-seek about death. It assumes that for the believer there is no real death. It is expected, perhaps, that the soul or reflexive self-awareness will detach itself from a body that is in pain and in distress over its vital functions. At a certain moment all pain ceases, there is light, and angelic singing is heard. The soul, continuing essentially the same life, is assured a heavenly welcome (a matter that is certain beforehand because it has kept the rules for entering into heavenly bliss). The path has been charted; it is all as expected. There are no surprises; it is all as the person has been taught beforehand and has believed. The whole model of expectations may not be exactly like this. Instead of continuous awareness there might be a "falling asleep" and reawakening into consciousness that mark the passage out of the body. There might be some fear in case the rules have not been kept well enough, or in case what has been believed is after all not entirely "true."

What seems so unfortunate about this type of attitude and expectation is that by denying the reality of death as the inscrutable mystery of human existence, it fails to call for a final consummation of the life project in charity. It seems to do rather the opposite, namely to focus attention on the self and the reward for the self. But salvation cannot come by making oneself the goal and purpose of life. It might be somewhat alleviated by the desire to be "with God," but it does not place the same radical exigence on the personal focus of the dying person as is placed by death seen as reality.

The third attitude is one that combines the atheist's ruthless awareness of the inscrutable finality of death with the believer's all-consuming response of praise and gratitude to God whose being and love is reflected in the believer's own maturity of being that overflows for others. It is the attitude of one who dies knowing that we do not really know what resurrection or heaven means or in what sense we personally participate in it, "what is in it for us," but facing death with total trust in God, and making a total surrender of oneself to God. The obvious exemplars of such a death are the martyrs who have chosen to die for a cause which simply matters to them more than anything they could claim for themselves. But such deaths are not limited to martyrs for a cause, much less limited to martyrs for the faith. Such deaths are, perhaps, not so uncommon among believing and prayerful Christians; many of our grandmothers, who slipped away in old age having grown into the habit of spending themselves totally for others and quietly enjoying it, must have died salvific deaths like this shaped by their enjoyment of, and their own reflection of, the love of God that had relativized everything else for them. But to die like this, as Christian spirituality has long reminded us, is generally given at the end of life to those who, in the sense of relativizing all to the call of charity, have been dying for a long time during their lives.

Notes

1. Karl Rahner, *On the Theology of Death.* N.Y.: Seabury, 1973.

2. Ladislas Boros, *The Mystery of Death.* N.Y.: Herder, 1965; *Living in Hope.* N.Y.: Herder, 1970.

3. Roger Troisfontaines, *I Do Not Die.* N.Y.: Desclee, 1963.

4. Norbert Greinacher and Alois Mueller, eds., *The Experience of Dying.* N.Y.: Herder, 1975.

5. Elisabeth Kübler-Ross, *On Death and Dying.* N.Y.: Macmillan, 1969.

6. See case histories in Kübler-Ross, *op. cit.*

7. The theme is particularly dominant in Karl Rahner's writings, but occurs in all the authors mentioned in the preface and is, of course, a traditional theme in Christian spirituality.

8. See particularly "The Hermeneutics of Eschatological Assertions," *Theological Investigations.* Vol. IV. Baltimore: Helicon, 1966, pp. 323–346.

9. Hendrikus Berkhof, *Well-Founded Hope.* Richmond: John Knox Press, 1969.

10. See especially H. A. Williams, *True Resurrection.* N.Y.: Harper & Row, 1974.

11. See, for instance, Gregory Baum, *Man Becoming,* N.Y.: Herder, 1971, ch. IV.

12. See especially, Edward Schillebeeckx and Boniface Willems, eds., *The Problem of Eschatology.* N.Y.: Paulist, 1969.

13. This widely diffused effort is founded, for instance, on the evolutionary vision of Teilhard de Chardin. Cf., *e.g.,* Troisfontaines, *op. cit.*

14. See Josef Neuner and J. Dupuis, eds., *The Christian Faith.* Westminster: Christian Classics, 1975. And cf. earlier arrangement by Josef Neuner and Heinrich Roos as re-edited by Karl Rahner, *The Teaching of the Catholic Church.* N.Y.: Alba House, 1967.

15. See particularly his entry, "Eschatology" in *Sacramentum Mundi,* Vol. 2. N.Y.: Herder, 1968, pp. 242–246.

16. As given in Henricus Denzinger and Adolfus Schoenmetzer, eds., *Enchiridion Symbolorum definitionum and declarationum de rebus fidei et morum.* N.Y.: Herder, 1965.

17. The order followed is that of the Denzinger *Enchiridion,* "Index systematicus," L. 1–7, pp. 922–926. The content as given in this chapter is necessarily much abbreviated and much simplified. For full texts, see Denzinger numbers given in the "Index." For evaluation of selection made, cf. Rahner and Neuner, *op. cit.*

18. Cf. Neuner, *op. cit.*

19. Cf. Karl Rahner, entry "Hell," in *Sacramentum Mundi,* Vol. 3. N.Y.: Herder, 1969, pp. 7–9.

20. The major contemporary focus has been on this aspect, as exemplified by contemporary theology of hope, political theology, liberation theologies, etc.

21. Besides those mentioned in the introduction, especially worthy of note is an essay of J. B. Metz, "The Future in the Memory of Suffering," in *New Questions about God,* ed. J. B. Metz. N.Y.: Herder, 1972.

22. Cf. David Flusser, *Jesus.* N.Y.: Herder, 1969.

23. Already enshrined in the Creeds, this teaching is explicit or implicit in the definitions of each of the four great councils of the fourth and fifth centuries and continues to be maintained subsequently.

24. The question of the literal meaning of the empty tomb is disputed among Scripture scholars. See, e.g., Willi Marxsen, *The Res-*

urrection of Jesus of Nazareth. Phila.: Fortress, 1970; Raymond Brown, *The Virginal Conception and Bodily Resurrection of Jesus.* N.Y.: Paulist, 1973.

25. See, e.g., H. A. Williams, *op. cit.*

26. Cf. Karl Rahner, entry "Death," in *Sacramentum Mundi,* Vol. 2. N.Y.: Herder, 1968, pp. 58–62.

27. For a concise summary, see the entry "Resurrection," *Dictionary of Biblical Theology,* ed. Xavier Leon-Dufour. N.Y.: Desclee, 1967, pp. 436–441.

28. See Rahner, *op. cit.*

29. See, e.g., positions presented in *The Mystical and Political Dimensions of the Faith,* ed. Claude Geffre and Gustavo Guitierrez. N.Y.: Paulist, 1975.

30. E.g. in the work of Karl Rahner, Henri de Lubac, Piet Schoonenberg, Roger Troisfontaines, etc.

31. E.g., Baum, Berkhof, Boros, Williams, *op. cit.*

Suggestions for Further Reading

Some readers may be anxious to follow up this brief introduction with further reading in one or other direction. The following suggestions are divided by chapter, according to the main questions raised in each chapter.

Chapter 1

Probably most helpful in further reading related to this chapter are the writings of Elisabeth Kübler-Ross, including *On Death and Dying* (N.Y.: Macmillan, 1969) and subsequent writings. Also very helpful is *Death and Its Mysteries* by Ignace Lepp (N.Y.: Macmillan, 1968). Quite informative and reassuring about the experience of those who have lost consciousness and are on the threshold of death is *Life after Life* by Raymond A. Moody, Jr. (N.Y.: Bantam Books, 1975).

Some indications of the cultural variations in the way death is experienced are given in *The Experience of Dying,* edited by Norbert Greinacher and Alois Mueller (N.Y.: Herder, 1974).

Chapter 2

The outstanding contribution to this discussion is certainly the essay "The Hermeneutics of Eschatological Assertions" in *Theologi-*

cal Investigations, Vol. IV, by Karl Rahner (Baltimore: Helicon, 1966). It is, however, quite difficult reading for the lay reader in the field of theology. Somewhat the same explanation is expressed very clearly in *Man Becoming* by Gregory Baum (N.Y.: Herder, 1970). Chapter IV.

Helpful in a very gentle way in this context are the writings of Anglican monk H. A. Williams, especially *True Resurrection* (N.Y.: Harper & Row, 1974).

Chapter 3

The official Church teachings are most accessible to the non-theologian in the reference volume *The Christian Faith,* edited by Josef Neuner and Jean Dupuis (Westminster: Christian Classics, 1975) or in the earlier edition of this entitled *The Teaching of the Catholic Church,* edited by Josef Neuner and Heinrich Roos under the supervision of Karl Rahner (N.Y.: Alba House, 1967).

The material is also clearly and very concisely presented by Gregory Baum in "Eschatology" in *An American Catholic Catechism,* edited by George Dyer (N.Y.: Seabury, 1975). A low-key explanation in non-technical language is also available in *A New Catechism* (N.Y.: Seabury, 1967).

Chapter 4

The explanation of the New Testament message of the death and resurrection of Jesus is probably most helpfully given in *The Virginal Conception and Bodily Resurrection of Jesus* by Raymond Brown (N.Y.: Paulist Press, 1973). A standard exegete's study is *The Resurrection of Jesus of Nazareth* by Willi Marxsen (Philadelphia: Fortress, 1970). Also very helpful on the topic is *A New Catechism* (N.Y.: Seabury, 1967).

Chapter 5

The main points of this chapter are developed at some length by Karl Rahner in *On the Theology of Death* (N.Y.: Seabury, 1973), and by Ladislas Boros in *The Mystery of Death* (N.Y.: Herder, 1965).

The important practical implications of various ways of conceptualizing "life beyond death" and the relationship of the present to the "beyond death" are set out in *The Mystical and Political Dimensions of the Faith,* edited by Claude Geffre and Gustavo Gutierrez (N.Y.: Paulist, 1975).

Chapter 6

The continuity between present and future aspects of salvation is frequently stressed and exemplified in the writings and testimonies of the charismatic communities. This corresponds to the testimonies we find in the Acts of the Apostles of the New Testament, and those in the writings of the apostolic Fathers (available in a great number of translations and editions) which echo the understanding of the Church of the first few generations.

On patterns of complementarity in the process of salvation, the reader may be interested in the reflections offered in *The Eucharist and the Hunger of the World* by Monika K. Hellwig (N.Y.: Paulist, 1976).

Conclusion

The spiritual literature of Christians through the centuries is full of testimonies and reflections on the dying of a Christian death.

Particularly helpful are autobiographies of the saints, as well as some of the better biographies that have been written about them with full respect for the truth and a sense of cultural and historical context. The Acts of the martyrs of the early ages contain a profound theology of Christian death but are written in a literary genre that requires some introduction.

Selected Bibliography

A. On the Experience of Death

Greinacher, Norbert, and Alois Mueller, eds. *The Experience of Dying.* N.Y.: Herder, 1974.

Kübler-Ross, Elisabeth, *On Death and Dying.* N.Y.: Macmillan, 1969.

Moody, Raymond A., *Life after Life.* N.Y.: Bantam Books, 1975.

B. On Christian Individual Eschatology

Baum, Gregory, *Man Becoming.* N.Y.: Herder, 1970, Chapter IV.

Berkhof, Hendrikus, *Well-Founded Hope.* Richmond, Va.: John Knox Press, 1969.

Boros, Ladislas, *The Mystery of Death.* N.Y.: Herder, 1965. *Living in Hope.* N.Y.: Herder, 1970.

Charles, R. H., *Eschatology.* N.Y.: Schocken, 1963.

Durrwell, F. X., *The Resurrection.* N.Y.: Sheed & Ward, 1960.

Marxsen, Willi, *The Resurrection of Jesus of Nazareth.* Philadelphia: Fortress Press, 1970.

Rahner, Karl, *On the Theology of Death.* N.Y.: Seabury, 1973. *Theological Investigations,* Vol. IV. Baltimore: Helicon, 1966, Part VI.

Schillebeeckx, Edward, and Boniface Willems, eds., *The Problem of Eschatology.* N.Y.: Paulist, 1969.

Theurer, Wolfdieter, ed., *Readings in Christian Eschatology.* Derby, N.Y.: Society of St. Paul, 1966.

Troisfontaines, Roger, *I Do Not Die.* N.Y.: Desclee, 1963.

Williams, H. A., *True Resurrection.* N.Y.: Harper & Row, 1974.